THE 5 KEY SUCCESS FACTORS OF BUSINESS

A POWERFUL SYSTEM FOR TOTAL BUSINESS SUCCESS

E.W. 'BUCK' LAWRIMORE

THE 5 KEY SUCCESS FACTORS OF BUSINESS
A POWERFUL SYSTEM FOR
TOTAL BUSINESS SUCCESS

Copyright 2024 by E. W. "Buck" Lawrimore

Approlia Publishers
1320 Fillmore Ave., Suite 312
Charlotte NC 28203 USA
www.Approlia.com

ISBN: 9798884529441

Printed in the United States of America

Second Edition, 2024.
The First Edition of this book, published in 2011, was titled
The 5 Key Success Factors: A Powerful System For Total Business Success

Disclaimer

The author is providing this book and its contents on an "as is" basis and makes no representations or warranties of any kind with respect to this book or its contents. The author disclaims all such representations and warranties, including but not limited to warranties of business success, personal success or well-being of any kind. Your success depends on actions you take, the overall operating environment, and many other factors beyond the author's control.

In addition, the author assumes no responsibility for errors, inaccuracies, omissions, or any other inconsistencies herein. The purpose of this book is to educate and inform the readers of possibilities for their lives. If you discover any errors or inaccuracies, please notify the author through his website BuckLawrimore.com.

In addition to earning royalties from the sales of this book, the author may also earn affiliate commissions on sales from other products provided by Amazon and other companies. This is no way has influenced the content of this book.

Table of Contents

Introduction: The Secrets Of Business Success

The difference between success and failure

"What are the most important factors that enable one business to succeed while others stumble or fail?"

Since the early 1980s and the publication of *In Search of Excellence* by Tom Peters and Bob Waterman, thousands of authors, professors, and consultants – including me – have attempted to answer that question. What makes this so challenging is to identify business success factors that:

- Work effectively for *a wide variety of organizations*, not just Fortune 500 companies with huge budgets, but for any small-to-midsize business, nonprofit or government organization
- *Really make a difference* in improving tangible results, such as increased income and profits, customer loyalty and retention, employee satisfaction and performance, quality, and operations improvement
- Will *stand the test of time* – not be the fad of the moment or the flavor of the month, and therefore...
- Are *grounded in concrete reality* and lasting truths, not just personal or subjective ideas.

Please note: This is not a book about everything you need to know to start and run a business, although there are some tips on starting a business in the Appendix. And this is not a bunch of ideas from someone who made millions of dollars growing a business their way. No, this book is very focused (see the 4 bullet points above), very objective and very realistic. It's also concise – about 100 pages, which you can read quickly and benefit from for a lifetime.

The sources of these powerful business secrets

The 5 Key Success Factors of Business will reveal to you the powerful secrets of business success including management, marketing, finances and more. It is based on the author's 25-year study of the success secrets of market-leading companies as revealed in hundreds of books and articles, as well as the author's own real-world experience spanning more than 40 years as an agency president and business success consultant.

While some success secrets reported in academic literature and other sources apply mainly to huge Fortune 500 companies, all the secrets and strategies that you read in this book are adapted for small to midsize businesses, who are the clients we worked with for many decades.

When you are being paid to help a business be more successful like I was, you had better know what you are doing and be good at it. Clients really hate it when you charge them a lot of money and they don't see increased income or profits in return. That cold, hard reality drove me to constantly read, learn and practice the most effective business principles as set forth in this book.

One day a client of mine, president of a local architectural firm, asked me if I would speak to the Charlotte chapter of the American Institute of Architects. When I asked him, "What about?" He answered, "Whatever you think would be most valuable."

For years I had been researching the "success secrets" of market-leading companies and had shelves full of books on that topic. I began flipping through their tables of content and found that each one had 5, 8, 10, 12 or more "key success factors" (by various names) which their authors had decided were most important or valuable. So, I started entering them into a spreadsheet, and after a few hours had collected 120 success factors.

I knew that was way too much for a 20-minute lunch talk, so I began combining them into various "buckets" or categories. A couple of hours later, I had combined them all into five major "key success factors": strategy, people, marketing, operations and finance.

A *factor* is "a circumstance, fact, or influence that contributes to a result or outcome." It's something that makes something else happen. In this book, we are going to explore the key factors that contribute to or drive business success. Not just little things but the most important things – what are called *key success factors* or critical success factors. These are the big things that make a big difference – that drive increased sales, market share, customer satisfaction, employee retention, operational excellence and more.

But of course, telling you five "secret words" is not going to be of much help in enhancing the success of your existing or planned business. Instead, you will find that each key success factor is composed of about 10 *principles* or guides for action, things that you *can* use to reliably strengthen your business success.

Definition of success factor

We might define "success factor" as "one of several elements that consistently cause or produce success in any business or organization." Implicit in this definition is the important awareness that *one* success factor by itself will NOT cause full success, any more than pure sugar will make a cake. Instead, just as with a good recipe, success factors must be combined in the right combinations to yield successful results.

After studying many lists of success factors by different authors and "experts" as noted above, including my own real-world business consulting experience, I was finally able to cut to the core of why certain success factors are essential for any business or organization. The reason is, quite simply, because they reflect the very nature of what a business or organization is and does. Here's how this works:

- Every organization is composed of **people** (employees, associates, managers etc.) and **things** (offices, equipment, money etc.).
- Every organization engages in **activities** which are **internal** and **external**.
- Every organization has a **focus** or **purpose** (like making money or serving the public).

But it is not just the **existence** of these factors that ensures success. They **exist** in all organizations, by definition. It is the **management** of these factors, how they are used, that ensures success. To turn organizational factors like those above into success factors, we need to use more business-like language. Keep in mind the very simple, realistic foundation of these success factors as described above, and they will be like your anchor in the storm, or a house built on rock. Each of these success factor names is **symbolic** – no one word captures all the dimensions of each factor, but the words I have chosen are simple, widely used, and easy to understand. Just remember not to oversimplify as you think about and use them.

1. **Strategy** – Maintaining a distinctive focus and purpose, including internal elements such as core values, and external elements such as market strategy and strategic planning; managing the business as a whole
2. **People** – Your employees and personnel within the business, or as this function is often called, human resources, including training and learning
3. **Operations** – Your internal activities, what your people do all day
4. **Marketing** – Your external activities, much more than selling to customers, as we will discuss
5. **Finances** – Not just your money but your equipment, furnishings, facilities and all the other "things" your company owns or leases

Success factors and living systems

Now it is extremely important to understand that these 5 Key Success Factors are not a hierarchy – I could have put any one of them first. I put strategy first because it gives purpose to all the other factors and sets direction for the business as a whole.

One problem with writing in a book is that it is linear – one word follows another, so lists are a natural way of writing. But lists do not exist in the real world. Instead, the real world is composed of what are called **living systems**. So just as important as the **identity** of the 5 Key Success Factors is the **relationships** between them – they are **interactive** and **interdependent**.

For example, your body is a living system. Take away your heart and blood vessels, or your brains and nerves, or your bones, or your internal organs, and you are no longer living and you're no longer a complete system. Just as the human body is an incredible system of millions of interactive parts, all essential for survival, an organization is even more incredible because it is composed of *multiple* humans, with people inside the organization interacting with customers and others outside the organization.

Understanding how all these different systems are connected and inter-dependent in larger systems is called the **systems perspective** or **systems thinking**, and is tremendously important for achieving and sustaining success in the 21st Century. That's because the Internet, the global economy, mobile phones, television and other forms of communication interconnect all of us as individuals and organizations, interactively and interdependently. You can't understand anything in isolation. It must be viewed as part of a living system, and a system of systems, that is truly global today. Systems thinking and systems perspective are not mentioned in most business books, but we have made them important in *The 5 Key Success Factors of Business* book because every business is a system operating among other systems.

The Star Model of Success Factors

From the systems perspective, we can view the 5 Key Success Factors through this "star model," which shows each success factor in relationship with every other success factor:

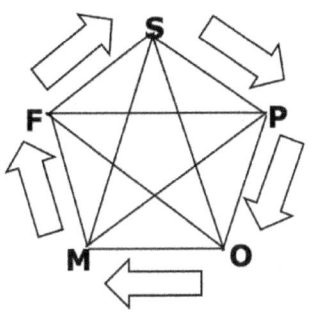

What does this model suggest? Three important things:

1. The 5 factors are interdependent, and the "model" can be rotated in any direction so that any factor appears "on top" at any time

2. There is a natural, predominant flow as strategy determines the people you need, who engage in operations to meet the needs of markets, which in turn generates finances that enable the continuing implementation of the strategy.

3. But "flow" is not just circular. Every factor is necessarily interconnected to every other factor, not just individually but collectively, meaning that there are actually 5 X 4 = 20 interrelationships to consider at any time. (Technically the total is more like 5X4X3X2 = 120, but we let's keep it simple for now.)

In fact, one of the biggest causes of failure in business and government is viewing people and situations as isolated objects, without understanding how everything is connected. I find it quite helpful, when I get into situations that are complicated and hard to understand, to fall back on the 5 Key Success Factors. They can be very useful tools for getting a handle on almost any problem or challenge. That's because they are rooted and grounded in concrete reality – people and things, internal and external activities, purpose or focus, as explained earlier.

Again, it's not the factors themselves that ensure success, but *how you use them*. To use them, you rely on key success *principles*.

Success factors and principles

Success factors are big powerful influences that make things happen, that drive business success in a big way. But they are not monolithic – they are not big "stones" made up of one thing. They are made up of **principles**. A principle is "an accepted or professed rule of action or conduct; a fundamental, primary or general law or truth from which others are derived."

As you may know, Elon Musk, one of the world's richest people, attributes his success in SpaceX, Tesla and other ventures to beginning with what he calls "first principles." These are the bedrock truths that he builds a business on.

Likewise Ray Dalio, one of the most successful hedge fund managers in America, wrote a book entitled *Principles* in which he explained the principles that he has used to drive his phenomenal success. (I believe the principles in the *5 Key Success Factors* book are more practical and useful for a typical small-to-midsize business, but I recommend Dalio's book if you are into high finance or high tech.)

Isaac Newton's famous book that lay the foundation for mathematical physics was called *Principia Mathematica* (mathematical principles).

The word *principle* is based on the Latin word for first or most important. If you want your business to be more successful, you will operate it using the foundational principles in this book, and others, all clustered into Key Success Factors, all connected into Living Systems. Got it?

So now let us look at each of the 5 Key Success Factors and the principles that each one involves. I begin with Strategy because, properly understood and implemented, it drives all the others.

Key Success Factor No. 1: Strategy

Strategy is based on the ancient Greek word for military general (*strategos*). A general thinks big-picture about all the forces at his disposal and all the challenges presented by the opposition, and develops a plan for victory, then commands the troops in battle to ensure that plans are followed and to adapt quickly to unexpected changes.

In addition to warfare, strategy is just as important in achieving success in business, athletics, non-profit management, and many other realms of life. You are the general of your business. That doesn't mean you bark at your employees like boot camp soldiers, but it does mean that you are responsible for everything that happens, good or bad. You are "the man" or "the woman" in charge. So it's vital that you understand, develop and enact an effective strategy for your business – not all by yourself, but in collaboration with your leadership team or your entire workforce.

Here are 10 key Principles of successful business strategy:

1. Leaders and managers are hard-working and capable.

The most important strategic success factor for every business is strong leadership:

- Leaders who have the necessary knowledge and skill for the business focus, industry or category
- Leaders who are able to inspire and encourage employees
- Managers who can make tough decisions and set priorities
- Leaders and managers who are willing to work hard and set an example of hard work for others to follow.

Managers versus leaders

Management and leadership are often used interchangeably, but they are different in important ways.

- Management is the process of planning, organizing, directing, and controlling resources to achieve specific goals. A manager is responsible for maintaining the existing systems, processes, and structures within an organization.

- Leadership, on the other hand, is the ability to inspire and guide individuals or groups towards a common goal or vision. A leader is someone who is able to influence and inspire others to achieve something that they might not have thought possible.

Some key qualities of a manager include:

- Being organized
- Being able to delegate tasks
- Being able to make decisions
- Being able to plan and budget

Some key qualities of a leader include:

- Being able to inspire and motivate others
- Having a clear vision
- Being able to communicate effectively
- Being able to think creatively and strategically

Sometimes both, sometimes not

Good leaders often possess many of the qualities of good managers, and vice versa, and in many cases, people in leadership roles also manage people and resources. However, importantly, some leaders are not cut out to be managers, and vice versa. I have worked with hundreds of companies over four decades and have found the manager-leader difference to be an important issue in a number of cases – often one that is not talked about because no one wants to openly criticize the top person.

Get to know your leadership strengths

If you are a manager or leader of a business, or want to become one, I urge you to explore your management and leadership strengths so you have an objective awareness of your strengths and any shortcomings. You can learn a lot by taking some free online tests (there are no right or wrong answers, only results that aid your self-understanding). Three you can take for free are:

- A free version of the Myers-Briggs type (personality) indicator; my current favorite is Truity.com, where it is called TypeFinder. Here's a link in this endnote:[1]
- The Big 5 personality test, also available at the Truity link for free
- The free VIA Character Strengths test at VIAcharacter.org.
- One more good one, not free, is the Clifton Strengths test designed to assess business-related strengths, originally developed by the Gallup Organization, at CliftonStrengths.com

Great leaders work hard

Over and over again, successful business executives say "hard work" was their key to success.

Elon Musk, who at the time of this writing had founded PayPal, SpaceX, Tesla and several other companies, was one of the wealthiest people in the world. But the beginning of his business success story began at a much lower level with extremely hard work.

He had learned computer programming on his own while a young teen in South Africa. He and his brother Kimball moved to Silicon Valley to seek their fortunes. He worked for a few startups but could not get a full-time job like he wanted. So he and his brother rented – not a small apartment but a small office, where they lived and worked 24-7. Initially they showered at the local YMCA, but basically Elon lived at his desk while his brother worked on sales.

They produced a small business-locator, money-making website called Zip2. (Think of it as an early version of Google Maps for business.) In the daytime their site was online making money, and in the evening they took it offline so they could improve it through more programming.

Eventually the company attracted investor capital, then was sold to Compaq Computers, making Musk millions of dollars. This gave him the cash he needed to start Paypal, which he later sold for $1.5 *billion* to eBay. He wanted to get into the space business, so he started SpaceX and worked hard learning how to be a rocket engineer. He later founded the electric vehicle company Tesla, which was so successful he became the wealthiest man on earth, worth more than \$275 billion before losing millions in Tesla stock value but still one of the top three billionaires in the world.

Musk is a modern counterpart to the great inventor Thomas Edison, who invented electric batteries, the light bulb, the phonograph, the motion picture projector and other electrical devices we take for granted today. His teachers said he was "too stupid to learn anything," and he was fired from his first two jobs for being "non-productive." But in fact, Edison worked so hard, he made 1,000 unsuccessful attempts at inventing the light bulb before he found the right filament material. He practically lived in his laboratory, just as Musk lived in his office.

Look at the background and practices of almost any successful person, including Bill Gates, Oprah Winfrey, Rupert Murdoch and countless others, and you will find they all credit their success to hard work.

Why hard work is so important

Why is hard work the No. 1 principle of business success? Here are a few reasons:

- Business is very competitive. To be successful, you must often outperform the competition, which is already entrenched, and once they see you in the arena, they may come after you. Beating the competition takes hard work.

- Business requires laser-like focus. You can't be all things to all people or jump on the fad of the day. You have to focus, focus, focus. This takes hard work.

- To be successful, a business must attract many paying customers. Not one or a few, but many. Each customer acquisition takes work, and acquiring many takes hard work.

- Almost no one starting a business knows how to run a business successfully. Because of what they don't know, they are likely to make many mistakes. As this book explains, at least five key success factors and 50 different action principles are involved in developing and sustaining a successful business. That takes hard work.

- Building a successful business requires attracting, training and retaining competent people. The bigger the business, the more people required, as a general rule. The more people you have, the more problems you have due to internal conflicts, jealousies, psychological problems and more. Making a team of people work like champions takes very hard work.

- And so it goes. All of the 50-plus success principles outlined in this book require hard work. You can read a book and *know* about them. You have to *work hard* to put them all into practice. Hard work is the No. 1 key to business success.

- BUT…. But… hard work alone will not ensure your success. You also have to work *smart* and be lucky, at least lucky enough that a natural disaster, competitor innovation or shifting consumer tastes don't wipe your business out. Companies that made buggy whips went out of business when consumers started buying automobiles. You can't control those external events, but you can learn to work smart… by reading the rest of this book and putting it into practice!

2. Focus on what you do best, a sustainable competitive advantage.

The most effective strategy in business as in athletics and war is to ***concentrate your resources on your greatest opportunities***. And your greatest opportunities are to ***build on your strengths which competitors cannot match***, while focusing on target markets you can dominate. This is called a ***sustainable competitive advantage***.

As one expert has said, "Define a niche small enough that you can dominate it." Maybe you can't run the best bakery in your city, but you can run the best bakery in your neighborhood. And this advantage must be sustainable in that it is rooted in who you are and what you do best, not some technology you bought off the shelf yesterday. This competitive advantage is closely connected to your core values and what your customers want the most from you, as noted in the next principle.

3. Build your business on what customers value most, driven by objective research.

Many business owners make the mistake of assuming that what they like, customers will also like. Far too many entrepreneurs invest incredible time, effort and money to launch a business selling what the *owners* like (but not the customers), and this is a major reason why so many young businesses fail.

Every city or town has small businesses such as antique shops, food specialty stores and home furnishings boutiques founded by people who wanted to turn their hobby or passion into a business. But not everyone shares that passion – in fact there may be so few people sharing it that there is no way this business can survive (unless it is propped up by a spouse or investor who makes lots of money elsewhere).

In reality, everyone is different, and you want to meet the needs of as many customers as possible who want your kind of products or services. This is essential to generate enough revenue to pay your bills and keep your business surviving and thriving without depending on a spouse's or "sugar daddy's" separate pool of money.

In other words, to strengthen and grow your business, it doesn't help much to focus on what you as the leader, manager or owner like. What matters most is to focus on what *the customer values most*. And in most cases, you can't get that information reliably by guessing or even by asking customers, who tend to tell you what they think you want to hear ("Yes, everything is fine") rather than what they really think or feel.

The best results by far are achieved through an objective survey administered by an experienced market research firm. If you don't think you can afford that, contact a local college or university that teaches marketing or business, and see if a class or group of students would be interested in doing a customer survey for little or no cost. This is discussed more in the chapter on marketing.

4. Define and share your authentic core values.

Core values are powerful statements of what you and your team passionately believe are most important in your business. These can't be glib, generic statements like "quality, price and service." They need to be the authentic words, thoughts and feelings of the leadership as well as the people of the organization.

Here for instance is a core value from a company I worked with: "Our processes must operate in a way that meets or exceeds current best practices of health and safety in our industry."

If you are not comfortable crafting your own core values internally, hire an expert to help you through this important process. If you have a limited budget, see if the local chapter of SCORE (Service Corps Of Retired Executives) has someone who will help you through this important step for free.

"Walk the talk."

It's not enough to paste your core values on the wall or hand them out on the back of business cards. Your people will know you really believe in those values when they see you talking about them naturally as you "manage by walking around" and work with others to solve problems. If you never talk about them, you communicate that they are just "words on paper." Use the values every day to demonstrate your commitment and strengthen their adherence within your organization.

5. Clarify your purpose with an inspiring, tangible vision and mission.

A vision statement is a picture of what you want your organization to be, look like and act like in the future, say 5 or 10 years out. A mission statement is what you *must do* to achieve that vision. State the vision in the present tense to make it tangible and believable. For example: "We are the leading health care architect in the Southwest." Your mission would then become monitoring the rapid changes in the health care field, designing new and better solutions to meet those needs, and promoting them throughout the Southwest through smart marketing, giving talks at professional meetings, producing white papers and more.

Like your core values, your vision and mission statements need to be demonstrated through daily action, involvement in group decisions, strategic choices and other important decisions.

6. Support your mission with achievable stretch goals.

If your company is generating $500,000 a year in sales, it is not much of a stretch to aim for a 10% increase in the following year. A stretch goal would be more like $1 million in sales. Good stretch goals stretch your organization to perform at its best but not "break" under too much stress and pressure.

The best goals are SMART goals – Specific, Measurable, Achievable, Realistic and Timed. But SMART goals can still be easy even if they are clearly defined. It is your job as a leader to stretch your team to its highest performance and win the equivalent of your championship or Super Bowl.

7. Back each goal with a clear action plan.

A goal is only as good as an action plan to achieve it. It needs to be supported with a clear, believable, how-to strategy like "We are going to hire 10 more salespeople and increase our marketing budget 35%." Then these specific strategies need to be translated into tactics – what are we going to do week by week, who is going to be responsible, how are we going to measure progress, and where is the work being done. Like goals, the tactics also need to be SMART.

A good guide or checklist for developing action plans is the 5W2H formula used by news reporters (like I used to be):

- **Who** is involved or responsible
- **What** are they going to do
- **When** are they going to do it
- **Where** are they going to do it
- **Why** are they going to do it
- **How** are they going to do it
- **How** much is it going to cost or earn?

You can also do online searches for solutions to your problems if you state them in the right words. Almost everything you can think of has already been done by someone and reported on some website.

8. Measure progress toward goals with a system guiding daily actions.

Many companies develop strategic plans or operating plans and put them on a shelf or in a file folder where they just gather dust, like pictures of your high school reunion. No real value for daily action. Unless you run a huge corporation, try to keep your goals list so simple that it and the supporting action plans can fit on one sheet of paper. Bring it to every staff meeting to guide discussion and decision-making. Once again "walk the talk."

If measuring progress seems difficult, think of the incredible volume of statistics generated in a three-hour professional football game! A system guiding daily actions can generate all kinds of measurements and data that can be used as feedback to continuously improve as well as to hit those stretch goals. "You can't manage what you can't measure" is an old saying that makes a valid point. You might not be able to measure everything with a number, but you can chart progress with subjective perceptions.

For example, a scale from 1 to 10 is commonly used by many physicians to ask patients what level of pain they are experiencing. The doctor can't stick a pain "scope" into your head to measure it objectively. And one person's "5 pain" may be another person's "10 pain." Still, the patient is the measurement point, and over time her judgment of her pain can become a valid tool for measuring change or no change.

In like manner you can ask your team members or customers questions that can be answered with numbers which, although subjective, over time provide valuable guidance and feedback.

9. Communicate all strategic objectives and plans frequently and update them regularly.

While it is ideal to update your strategic action plans continuously as situations change, at least once a year set aside time for a major review from top to bottom — values, vision, mission, goals, strategies, tactics. Create a system that works like a well-oiled machine and can be constantly improved year after year. Once you reach your first stretch goals, set another group of goals, so you continue to stretch further and achieve more.

The Japanese have long advocated a process known as *kaizen*, which means continuous improvement. By identifying and making one small improvement after another, the overall results can be quite remarkable.

Now somewhere in all this strategic planning and implementation, there will surely arise some confidential information such as personal salaries or problem individuals who may need to be let go. But that kind of personal issue should not get in the way of the primary objective and value of constantly sharing all key strategic information with as many people as possible. Even basic line workers need these strategies and plans translated into language they can understand so they can be supportive as well. Like a big rowboat, everyone needs to be pulling in the same direction.

'What we've got here is failure to communicate'

That line from the classic Paul Newman movie *Cool Hand Luke* expresses the prison guard's frustration over Newman's character not obeying orders, so he whacks him with a club. But it has become an oft-repeated expression of failure to communicate at all levels in corporate America.

My company conducted many surveys and focus groups of employees of different organizations. In almost every case, the rank-and-file people complain of poor internal communication. Leaders don't let them know what is going on to their satisfaction. The non-leaders often work with painfully limited information. The organization is not functioning as a true living system – it is just functioning as a bunch of people under one roof.

This takes us back to the great importance of strategy as shared purpose, focus, vision and values. The more such key directional elements are truly shared, the more the organization *can* act as one united system. Not only is information shared about what is going on daily and hourly, but also information is shared about what is going on monthly, annually and long-term. The organization knows what it is and where it is going.

When this sense of purpose and vision are really "alive" within each member of the organization, its success is not so dependent on the leaders at the top. It's more like a starfish that can regenerate a limb if one is cut off. The organization is a true whole, and the whole is greater than the sum of the parts. The whole has a life of its own and is thus more resilient and more likely to succeed in bad times as well as good.

Measure progress toward key goals all the time

A major reason most strategic plans fail is because they are thick documents that (a) people can't keep in their heads and (b) can only be changed once a year or longer — when in reality some kind of change happens weekly if not daily to many organizations.

In the 21st Century, organizations are increasingly measuring their progress toward a few key goals all the time. A number of businesses and organizations have adopted *The Balanced Scorecard* (see the book by that name for details). It emphasizes measuring four key areas of progress (this language from the first edition has evolved over time):

- **Learning & Growth** (human resource development, employee satisfaction, information systems etc.)
- **Internal Business Processes** (quality control, cycle time etc.),
- **Customers** (satisfaction, market share etc.), and
- **Financial** (income, profits etc.).

One point well made by *The Balanced Scorecard* is: If you are only measuring financial results, you are using *past-performance* data and "driving by looking in the rear-view mirror." Financial results are *lagging indicators* of progress. By contrast, Learning & Growth, Internal Business Processes and Customer Relations are *leading indicators* – they come *before* the profits are earned (or not).

Some companies benefit from an online "instrument panel" or "dashboard" of key measurements that are constantly updated to let team members know how the company is doing. This system is by definition objective, and it should be open to all key personnel. Even if you don't want to share all financial details, you can share a few key numbers like sales and profits for the month. Even more important is to measure other dimensions of performance that better enable you to predict the future rather than reflect the past. This is an important "missing element" of many strategic plans and one reason they do not work.

The newest approaches to these challenges shift the emphasis from an "instrument panel" which suggests machines measuring objects, to information and feedback, which are vital processes for all living systems. You as a living system yourself could not get along in the world without your senses giving you a constant flow of information and feedback from the environment in which you are living and moving. As we walk, for example, millions of signals are constantly flowing from our eyes, our feet, our ears, and other bodily parts, helping us keep our balance, move in the desired direction, and avoid obstacles.

In an organization like a business, we are all operating as individuals with all senses working, but one important thing is missing that keeps our group from functioning as a living system. Can you think of what that is?

What is missing is *a continuous flow of information and feedback* among the parts (people) in our system! Yes, we have email, meetings, conversations and other forms of communication. But one of the main reasons human organizations fail to achieve significant and enduring success is that "the left hand doesn't know what the right hand is doing."

One way to overcome that problem is to align all five success factors into a Strategic Management System, which is the tenth and final principle of the Strategy success factor.

10. Align all success factors in a realistic Strategic Management System.

We have identified five powerful success factors for business and organizations. But they cannot be treated as separate departments doing their own thing. They all need to be aligned in one system. They need to reinforce each other. The arm needs to know what the leg is doing, and the eye needs to know what the ear is doing, to use a "body" analogy.

It is the job of the strategic leaders of the organization to make sure everything is connected, works as one, works as a whole, so that the whole is greater than the sum of the parts. Results will then be truly outstanding, far greater than you ever believed possible.

Here are four ways to develop and improve your business's Strategic Management System:

1. Practice systems thinking for best results

Truly effective strategy in the 21st Century requires an appreciation of the living system perspective which we portrayed as a five-factor star model earlier. The organization is understood and managed as a dynamic, interconnected system, with interdependent parts acting as a whole. Peter Senge influenced many thousands of people with his 1994 best-seller, *The Fifth Discipline*, which strongly advocated *systems thinking*. (Systems thinking *is* the "fifth" discipline.)

In more recent years, more and more people and organizations have adopted the *living systems* perspective. The key difference is that earlier systems thinking was based on *mechanical paradigms* such as cause and effect, also called *linear thinking*, which tends to view the organization as a machine. The newer living systems view instead emphasizes that causes and effects are interactive and interdependent. For example, in human relationships it is often impossible to say "who struck first" but more helpful to look at the interaction. I relate to you in ways influenced by how you relate to me, which is influenced by how I related to you earlier, which was influenced by how you related to me earlier, and so on back to the very start of each relationship.

Another aspect of the living systems perspective is to view an organization as a living organism, struggling to survive in a sometimes-hostile environment. Some have used the analogy of an amoeba, which changes shape as needed to absorb food or avoid danger. But a true living system in the new view is composed of multiple individuals interacting in complex ways. The important point of this living systems view is that organizations consisting of multiple people are inherently complex, involving so many interactions and interdependencies that any attempt to restrict them with a "linear" process such as traditional strategic planning is bound to have shortcomings.

2. Engage in continuous learning

Living systems can adapt to the changing environment only because they have the capacity to *learn*. This is why Peter Senge and others have advocated the "Learning Organization." If your organization cannot *learn* from experience in the real world, it will repeat the same mistakes over and over, and is not likely to survive very long. Since people come and go in organizations, taking the learning out of people's heads and turning it into structures and processes is vitally important and valuable. (We talk about this more in the chapter on Operations.) This has given rise to the relatively new field of Knowledge Management. It seeks to capture the knowledge of the people in the organization and use it as a database to guide smarter decisions in the future.

You know for example whenever you call a company for technical support, 99% of the time the tech support person is reading answers from a database after entering a description of your problem. But this requires the resources of a fairly large organization and is not something most small businesses can sustain. However, as we will discuss in the chapter on Operations, any organization can write down its standard procedures so that everyone is on the same page, and key knowledge does not go out the door whenever an employee leaves.

3. Constantly adapt to the changing environment

At the very least, successfully adapting to the changing environment, which is so essential to success in the 21st Century, does require *observing* the environment and talking about it within the management team. This in turn requires reading online and offline news media, going to professional association meetings and trade shows, keeping a finger on the pulse of the marketplace and the competition. Often this happens informally, as one person will tell another something he observed or learned about. But if it is formalized in the sense of being regularly discussed at management meetings, put in writing, and shared internally, the power of continuous adaptation can be made much more effective.

Human communication is so difficult, the only way to avoid costly mistakes is to *over-communicate*, especially on critical projects or processes. A central shared database, password-protected, is one way to do that. But most small organizations don't have the manpower to sustain that. Instead, all of us can keep in mind this important truth: the greater the possibility of *misunderstanding*, the more important *face-to-face* communication becomes. Some experts claim that 80 percent of effective interpersonal communication is non-verbal! Often body language, facial expression, tone of voice and other non-verbal cues communicate more than just words on paper or email.

4. Check interrelationships with other success factors

Finally, as a checklist for ensuring effective 21st-Century strategy, consider its interrelationships with the other Key Success Factors with questions like these:

1. Has our strategy been created with the full involvement of our **people**, and does it reflect what they care about and are committed to?
2. Has our strategy been created with the full involvement of our **markets**, with objective research or surveys into the needs, perceptions and preferences of customers, prospects, and others outside of the organization?
3. Have we thought through the **operational** aspects of implementing our strategy on a day-to-day basis, so it becomes a part of our on-going work and internal processes?
4. Have we considered the **financial** aspects of our strategy, how we are going to pay for these initiatives, and how we are going to ensure the continuing financial strength of the organization? Does our strategy include considerations for our facilities, equipment, and pay structure?

So, to summarize, the Strategy Success Factor has several key components which, united into a system, keep the organization on track, keep everyone singing off the same page, keep customers happy, keep competitors in the dust, keep the money rolling in, keep the profits up. That's why we consider Strategy the No. 1 Key Success Factor.

Key Success Factor No. 1: Strategy – Chapter Summary

1. Leaders and managers are hard-working and capable.
2. Focus on what you do best, a sustainable competitive advantage.
3. Build your business on what customers value most, based on objective research.
4. Define and share your authentic core values.
5. Clarify your purpose with an inspiring, tangible vision and mission.
6. Support your mission with achievable stretch goals.
7. Back each goal with a clear action plan.
8. Measure progress toward goals with a system guiding daily actions.
9. Communicate all strategic objectives and plans frequently and update them regularly.
10. Align all success factors in a realistic Strategic Management System.

Key Success Factor No. 2: People

How "people" are like the weather

"People" are a primary key to business success, as all we people know. But "people" as a success factor is often like the weather – everybody talks about it, but often no one does anything about it. Having worked with hundreds of business, government and non-profit organizations, I cannot tell you how many times I heard or read the statement, "What makes us different is our people" or "People are the key to our success."

Well of course they are. You can't have a business without people, and attracting and retaining good people is indeed vital for business success. But many different Principles are important in managing people for greater success. Here are 12 important and powerful Principles, all based on research and experience, for hiring and managing people in your organization:

1. Hire carefully based on talent and personal strengths.

In the real world, managers tend to hire people based not so much on their talent and personal strengths but on their job history, their appearance and whether they like them or not. They look at the resume, they look at the person, they check their gut, and think "yes" or "no." Research has shown that we all tend to develop a "like/don't like" impression of someone in the first few seconds in which we meet them. That is how the brain is hardwired for "approach/avoid" in the natural world. So you have to intentionally override that first impression and be open to learning more about the candidate.

According to research studies, talent and personal strengths are better predictors of future performance. But how do you judge talent? We're not talking about hiring singers or dancers in most business situations. And if I am hiring, say, a bookkeeper, I cannot ask the candidates, "Show me how you do bookkeeping" while you look over their shoulder. So you first have to consider what sort of talent is relevant for the job, then develop a way to check or test for it. One way to do this is to ask one or more people who have performed successfully in the job before, what kind of talent they think is needed, and what sort of questions you could ask to see how the candidate stacks up. Another is to do some online research for questions such as "What sort of talents are needed for bookkeeping?" You'll likely find plenty of relevant suggestions unless the job is really unusual.

Personal strengths can be judged by a wide range of standardized tests. My company used the Myers-Briggs Type Indicator for many years with highly useful results. You don't hire someone based solely on their personality type of course, but this can be one factor to consider along with their work experience, personal presentation and more. It's available free online at several sites. Other tests are called "strength finders" and offer a different but valuable perspective. If your company depends on a core talent or strength, you can also offer a test that you devise to see how the person performs for a specific assignment. For example, in my company writing talent was very important for writer-researcher positions. So I would sometimes give applicants a writing test that was similar to an assignment they might receive if they were working for us.

You might want to do the first round of testing just based on interviews, and after you identify one or more finalists, invite them back for the testing portion. Sometimes people can feel a little overwhelmed if they go to an interview, sit down with a stranger, then are asked to take any kind of "test." Whereas if you invite them back for a second meeting, you can explain that they have made a good first impression and now are advancing to the second round, so it appears to be a positive experience or recognition.

2. Organize your people with a structure that is clear yet adaptable to change.

Organizational structure tends to evolve over time in a business in a somewhat natural manner as different specializations are needed, or different tasks are encountered. In the beginning the founder does everything, but as he or she gets too busy to do it all, some work can be broken off and assigned to someone more specialized. The first person my company hired was a bookkeeper/receptionist because we needed someone to do both.

But the organization development does not always evolve in a productive manner. One of my clients was a chemical company who had departments for operations, finance, personnel and strategic management, but no one for marketing. They tried hiring some technical salespeople but that did not work. Marketing was never on a par with the other departments in the company.

The 5 Key Success Factors really are a good way to organize many different kinds of business because they are logical and based on the very nature of business, as noted earlier. They also serve as a good checklist because, if you don't have one of the factors covered by someone responsible, maybe now is the time to make that change.

And speaking of change, nothing is more important to the survival of your business in this constantly changing world we live in than rapid *adaptation* to change. Adapt or die, as one business leader said. In the natural world, the species that have survived the longest are the ones which adapted to their constantly changing environment. In the late 20th Century, some businesses adapted rapidly to the opportunities and challenges of the Internet, and some did not. No business did a better job of adapting than Amazon.com, which went from selling books online to music and electronics, and now sells just about anything in the world that can be packaged and shipped.

By contrast a large regional retailer in my area, where I used to buy most of my clothes before the Internet, was slow to develop e-commerce and never had a user-friendly website. Like many other brick-and-mortar stores, they are in financial trouble. Sears is another example of a department store chain that once was a huge business success, but never adapted well to the Internet and died a painful death.

As the business world evolves and becomes ever more complex, learn to embrace change so that you can adapt your structure and operations quickly to take advantage of new opportunities and enjoy ever-increasing success.

3. Give your people opportunities to develop their valuable skills and knowledge.

Just as a business must adapt to constant change, so must your people. Google expects its employees to spend 80 percent of their time serving the search engine giant, and 20 percent exploring new possibilities. That led to the development of Gmail, Adwords (paid advertising) and much more.

Too many companies just expect their people to work, work, work, and if they want to learn some new skills, they can do it on their own time. Others encourage employees to attend professional development meetings and seminars, to take online courses, or to participate in in-house "lunch and learn" events.

As noted in Chapter 1, the organization which makes constant learning a part of its very fiber has unlimited growth and success potential. This is why it's so valuable to not only allow but also encourage your people to be constantly developing their valuable skills and knowledge.

4. Be sure your people understand overall company strategy and what is expected of them.

It's a rare company that takes time and effort to explain to its employees the overall business strategy, priority and goals. How can you expect your people to all be pulling in the same direction if they don't know what the direction is? Note the words above, "Be sure your people understand." Don't bore them with corporate-speak about shareholder value, competitive benchmarking, business process management . . . blah, blah, blah.

Put your company story into language they can understand. The ideal scenario is to involve them initially in developing company strategy by asking for their ideas about what customers value most, what internal processes can be improved, and what sort of structural changes might make the company work better. Or give them our Key Success Factor Scorecard[2] so they can rate the company on about 50 different Principles. Then you can explore with them any Principles or areas that got low ratings, and why. Or you can use the aggregate information for an overall company improvement initiative such as a strategic plan or organization development.

Within this overall principle, nothing is more important than making sure each employee understands what is expected of them. People tend to do a job the way they want to, or the way they did it at another company, unless they are given clear instructions and explanations of what is expected of them in *this* job at *this* time.

All too often the employee who seems to be underperforming or drifting may not even realize she is off course because she really does not understand what is expected of her. Regular conversations between each employee and her supervisor can go a long way to minimizing these problems and maximizing success for all concerned.

5. Reward your people for desirable performance, individually and as a team.

Michael LeBoeuf wrote a highly regarded little book called, *The Greatest Management Principle in the World,* and this principle is, "That which gets reinforced gets repeated." This powerful reinforcement principle of psychology and human behavior was discovered by behavioral psychologist B.F. Skinner and has been rejected by some people because it applies as much to rats in a cage as it does to humans. And guess what? It works just as well on both (including kids).

If you want somebody to repeat a behavior, reinforce it with some type of reward that they will appreciate. That might be as simple as saying "Well done." If you want somebody to stop a behavior, withdraw the reinforcement. This leads (ideally) to what is called *extinction.* And interestingly, the most powerful way to *sustain* a behavior is through *intermittent* reinforcement. If a team member wants something that is not in the firm's best interests, and you give in just a couple of times, that habit will be more deeply ingrained than if you gave in every time, then suddenly stopped. Consistency is extremely important in shaping people's behavior.

There are several other key elements in rewarding desirable performance for effective results:

- **First of all, performance needs to be measured in some way.** We talked earlier about SMART goals and tactics. Some form of measurement needs to be established at the beginning of setting each objective. Once the form of measurement is established, such as billable hours per week, then you need to establish a numeric target, such as 80 percent. So in a 40-hour week, the target is to record at least 32 billable hours per week. That is a lofty goal but is used here just for illustration purposes.

- **Then each person and team needs to understand what they can do to meet or exceed the target.** For example it may not just be a matter of working hard but also working smart, to be sure effort is applied in the right direction. Billable hours require sufficient volume of pending work that every team member can focus on doing the work as needed. In reality it may be necessary for some team members or others in the organization to get more new business before everyone has even a chance to meet the target.

- **A reward program needs to be carefully constructed** so that positive behavior (quality and not just quantity) gets appropriately noted and recognized. In some cases this might be money, but studies have shown that people appreciate even more being recognized in front of the group. An honor like "Employee of the Month" can be a truly appreciated reward in some corporate cultures, and a meaningless time-waster if it is overdone. When an employee is recognized publicly with sincere, original praise from upper management, that can go a long way to reinforcing good behavior patterns for all participants.

- **Different strokes for different folks.** Because people are fundamentally unique individuals, what one considers a reward, another may consider punishment. This is related to the earlier principle of "motivating" people by focusing on their strengths and giving positive feedback. If you know your people's strengths or personality types, you can give them the strokes they want; if not, you run the risk of giving them strokes *against* their grain by treating them the way *you* want to be treated, not the way *they* want to be treated. This is also called the Platinum Rule: Do unto others as they want to be done unto.

6. Regularly survey your people about satisfaction and improvement ideas.

This is almost never done in small businesses, yet it can be so valuable. Management needs to consider employees as internal "customers" whose satisfaction is just as important as external customers. A simple one-page survey on paper or online can give the option of anonymity or name/email for those who are open to follow-up discussion. A numeric rating for satisfaction on key items such as these principles we are identifying in *The 5 Key Success Factors* book makes gathering and interpreting relevant data a valuable way to get actionable measurement and feedback. Or perhaps critical issues have been identified in previous strategic planning processes. Be sure to measure what is important and avoid mindless questions like, "What is your favorite color?"

7. Give your people autonomy to make decisions aligned with strategic goals.

People work more productively when given some freedom to make decisions in the moment, as needed. They don't want or need to stop every few minutes and ask a supervisor "Is this OK?" or "What should I do now?" But it isn't practical to give your people too much freedom – that can lead to costly mistakes and wasted time. So the right balance involves making sure they understand the organization's strategic goals so they can make decisions aligned with those goals. This may take some training – just telling someone "Here are our strategic goals" in no way ensures that they will consider those goals each time they make a decision at work. So that gets back to Principle 4, "Be sure your people understand overall company strategy and what is expected of them."

8. Motivate your people by focusing on their strengths and giving positive feedback.

Motivation is often misunderstood. Many people think it's like the football coach giving a rousing pep talk at halftime. But research has discovered that you cannot motivate someone from the outside very effectively. Motivation is internal, or "intrinsic" as it is called. If I am your manager, I have to "ring your chimes" by focusing on your own internal strengths and desires, on what you do best and what you want to do.

There are several online surveys or questionnaires that can enable each person to identify their strengths. One of the most widely used is the Myers-Briggs Type Indicator, which you can take for free on Truity.com[3] or other sites. Big 5 is another somewhat different assessment but less well known. And the people who wrote the book, *Now Discover Your Strengths*, while working for the Gallup Organization, have a current instrument called CliftonStrengths which you can also take online, but not for free.

In our organization and some clients we have worked for, each person's Myers-Briggs Type is known and shared with others. Every type has definite strengths which can be very valuable when used appropriately in the workplace. For example, people with the SJ preference are typically good at organizing, list-making, and in many cases accounting. We never hired a bookkeeper who was not an SJ.

By contrast you might have someone who has the NF preference, which is more creative-expressive. NFs are typically fun to be around and enjoy using their creativity in a wide range of fields from the performing arts to counseling others.

Once you know someone's natural strengths, you can make an effort to delegate work to them that will be a good fit. Then you can reward them with some type of recognition, from one-on-one to a group setting or financial perks, as a way of cementing your relationship with them and enhancing their job satisfaction. Several studies have found that most people enjoy public recognition more than money as a reward for desirable performance.

It's all about human energy.

Human energy is the ultimate resource for any business. People are not just bodies but *energy systems* with mental, physical, emotional and spiritual energies, all of which can be engaged or ignored. Any planning effort or change effort will succeed best if you channel people's natural energies in the direction of the new activities. Find out how each person naturally uses his or her energies through instruments like Myers-Briggs or Clifton-Strengths. Try to give them roles in the new activities that let them use their natural energies effectively. Communicate with them often – up-front and on-going. It is amazing what people will do when you work with their natural energies and encourage them along the way.

9. Keep everyone informed of new developments with frequent communications.

Almost every employee survey my firm has ever done, and this is probably true of many others, found that people on the lower rungs of the ladder feel that upper management does not do a good job of keeping them informed of new developments via frequent communications. All too often the new development is announced like this: "Jane, we are reassigning you to the widget division in North Boondocks effective Monday."

Now not every management decision-making process can be shared openly while it is going on. Some of these processes involve discussions about specific personnel that need to be kept confidential. Or in the case of a company considering relocating to several competing cities, it would lose leverage and possibly millions of dollars if the search process is shared openly with all personnel while it is going on. You have to use common sense here.

The point is to be considerate of your people who are not on the inside regarding new developments. Think about how they might be impacted as you work on your decisions. Look for ways to give them a heads-up that a new development is in the pipeline.

The best way to do that? Small group meetings. Emails and written memos are terrible at answering questions and providing reassurance. Plus they increase the risk that the information will be leaked to outsiders at the wrong time in the wrong way. Did you know that more than 80 percent of effective communication is non-verbal? The expression on your face, your body language, your tone of voice and more communicate feelings like confidence and caring in ways that words on paper or screens can never do. Yes, meetings can take longer than an email blast. But in the long run, that is one of the best investments you can make.

You cannot not communicate.

That axiom, from the classic little book *The Pragmatics of Human Communication*, refers to the fact that *not communicating* with someone says to them, "I don't care about you." When my firm did numerous studies of nonmanagerial employees, we *always* found that the employees consider internal communication to be inadequate. Managers get busy putting out fires and trying to be sure customers' needs are met, and they forget the importance of communicating with everyone about what's going on with the company. They may rationalize that by thinking, "I'm in charge and I know what I'm doing," but all the employees see is the stone wall of silence. This is an important component of Principle 9, "Keep everyone informed of new developments with frequent communications."

People want to know what is going on and how it does or will affect them, and you cannot overdo that or fake it. Open communication shows people you care about them. *Not* communicating says you *don't* care about them, even if you think you do.

10. Encourage people to cooperate with each other to achieve customer satisfaction.

"That's not my department" is a classic statement you don't want to hear in your organization. Your people need to understand that customer satisfaction is the top priority, and they need to work together to make that happen.

This is not natural for everyone. Some people, depending on their personality type, tend naturally to focus on their work, their responsibilities and their span of control. They like to work in a logical sequence of steps. So stopping their normal workflow to reach out to another department or worker to satisfy a customer just may not be natural for them. This can be especially challenging when confronted by an unhappy customer who makes a complaint. The tightly focused employee may also be conflict aversive and uncomfortable when someone attempts to lay the company's failures on their shoulders. "Nope, not my department."

Overcoming this natural isolating tendency requires training and retraining employees to think "as one" for the organization as a whole and to think about "lifetime customer value." A customer complaining about a $10 purchase may take their business elsewhere if not satisfied. But taking care of their concerns in a positive way – even if they are wrong – can make them a customer for life, resulting in hundreds or thousands of dollars in purchases over time.

If employees understand the connections between their behavior on behalf of the company as a whole, customer satisfaction, and company profits, each person's contribution can be multiplied many times over. But again people are not born understanding this, so they need to be educated and reminded on a regular basis.

11. Make sure people are open to change when new challenges or strategies require it.

Some people like change but many people dislike change, especially when they do not have a voice in the change decision. The old familiar routines are so comfortable, and workers like knowing what is expected of them and fulfilling those expectations consistently.

The ancient Greek philosopher Heraclitus is remembered for claiming, "No man ever steps in the same river twice, for it's not the same river and he's not the same man." The river in this case is world events – constantly changing as do we, men and women, young and old.

The world we live and work in during the 21st Century and beyond is constantly, rapidly changing. During the 2020s, a Coronavirus pandemic was sweeping the world and killing hundreds of thousands of people, at the same time that a contentious presidential election was ousting one party leader and inducting another, with great conflict along the way. Every day some new technology is announced — some of it beneficial for all of us, some of it threatening our job security.

Your people need to understand that sticking their heads in the sand and resisting change is counterproductive for them and for the company. If you all don't embrace change and work to stay on the leading edge, your competitors will outpace you, outperform you, and take away your customers and your income. Serious consequences.

Change driven by your own strategies are often in response to the external world and competition. Sustaining a competitive advantage means continuously running to stay in place.

We referred earlier to the little-known concept of organizations as living systems. In the natural world, organisms must adapt to the constantly changing environment or die. Thousands of animal species have become extinct because they could not or did not adapt to their changing environments. Even companies on the Fortune 500 die or lose power at an alarming rate. As of this writing, only 52 companies which were on the Fortune 500 in 1955 are still on it, due in part to what is called "creative destruction." Consider how Walmart destroyed many small-town merchants, or how Amazon's business model destroyed many brick-and-mortar stores. Your people need to understand that this economic process is a fact of business life, cannot be stopped, but instead needs to be understood as your team strives to adapt to its constantly changing environment.

You can't change people; change the system.

By the time someone is in their early twenties, their personalities and behaviors are so set that nothing is going to change *them* except a significant emotional event. Such an event might be marriage, divorce, the birth of a child, the death of a loved one, or getting fired from a long-held job. It is hard to engineer positive emotional events at work that are significant and appropriate. Some teams go whitewater rafting or wilderness hiking to share emotional experiences. But generally speaking, you cannot change people, so instead you change the system of rewards that reinforce desired behaviors, or in rare cases, punish unacceptable behaviors (generally punishment backfires and creates deep resentment, even rebellion).

For example, if quality is important, you create a *system* that measures and rewards high quality. You don't just preach to your people or put up signs that say, "Remember, don't make mistakes!" And you walk the talk by demonstrating your own passion for quality – or whatever behavioral change you are trying to instill.

12. Give all people real input into decisions or changes which affect them.

Many organizations work top-down, where all major decisions are made by upper management and announced to lower employees on an as-needed basis. This is a prescription for employee disappointment and in some cases dysfunction and turnover. Much better results will be attained if people who are going to be affected by a decision have real input into it. In my experience with hundreds of diverse organizations, this rarely happens.

Management might claim that lower employees do not or cannot understand the complex factors that go into making the right business decision. Or perhaps as the comic strip Dilbert often lampooned, management might make decisions based on whim, without logical reasons, and don't want to be challenged by the workforce.

The noted management guru and author Stephen Covey warned, "No involvement, no commitment." If people are not involved in making a decision, don't expect them to be committed to implementing it, especially if they think it is a dumb idea. But there's more to making a good decision than just asking people, "What do you think?"

Over the years I've been involved in a number of situations where employees' hopes were raised through focus groups or other input, but in spite of our recommendations, management did not act on what people said. Again you do not have to do what your people suggest. But employee emotions are extremely time sensitive. You lift their hopes when you seek their input, and if you act on that input, you sustain their enthusiasm and energies. If you wait too long, the emotional peak passes and you will not have another chance like that for a long time.

This is one reason GE had great success with their "workout" sessions in their glory days under CEO Jack Welch. Everyone involved gets in one room and one manager is in charge. Discussion focuses on one problem. No one leaves the room until the manager decides what action will be taken on the problem. The decision may be to act now or to delegate the problem to a task force if more information is essential, but some action is always taken. This is one way GE kept their people "generally electrified" and loyal.

The SimpleD Decision-Making Model

Based on years of research and experience, I developed the SimpleD (*pronounced Simple-D*) decision-making model that works in many diverse situations. I have explained it in depth in the Appendix of this book. Here's the process in a nutshell:

1. **S**ituation – Analyze the situation that the decision relates to in terms of who, what, when, where, why, how and how much.
2. **I**ntention – What purpose are you trying to accomplish, what values are relevant, and who should be included in the process (all people who might be affected by it, as noted above)?
3. **M**ultiple options – Generate several options as possible choices for outcomes of the decision-making.
4. **P**ros and cons – Evaluate each option in terms of pros and cons (this may require some additional fact-finding).
5. **L**ong view – Consider the long-term consequences of each option such as impacts on people, finances, competition, community and more.
6. **E**valuate each option now in terms of its pros and cons and possible long-term consequences.
7. **D**ecide – Choose the option that seems most promising, then move forward into action.

All too often decisions are made by individuals, companies and groups that do not consider relevant values, who should be included, clearly stated multiple options, comparative pros and cons, or long-term impacts. By rushing decisions or making them with the "gut," thousands and thousands of companies have suffered disastrous consequences. This is one reason even

Fortune 500 companies run off the rails and eventually die. You can do better with the SimpleD decision-making process!

Interrelationships with Other Success Factors

Finally, as a checklist for ensuring effective 21st-Century **people** management, consider its interrelationships with the other Key Success Factors with questions like these:

- Do our people understand our **strategy**, and has it been created or updated with the full involvement of our people, reflecting what they care about and are committed to?

- Do our people understand the needs of our **markets,** including objective research or surveys into the needs, perceptions and preferences of customers, prospects, and others outside of the organization?

- Do our people understand and support our **operations** and their role in the system, so that our work procedures provide consistent quality, price and service?

- Do our people understand overall company **finances** and their role in maintaining our profits and financial strength? Have we provided them with adequate facilities and tools to do their jobs well?

Key Success Factor No. 2: People – Chapter Summary

1. Hire carefully based on talent and personal strengths.
2. Organize your people with a structure that is clear yet adaptable to change.
3. Give your people opportunities to develop their valuable skills and knowledge.
4. Be sure your people understand overall company strategy and what is expected of them.
5. Reward your people for desirable performance, individually and as a team.
6. Regularly survey your people about satisfaction and improvement ideas.
7. Give your people autonomy to make decisions aligned with strategic goals.
8. Motivate your people by focusing on their strengths and giving positive feedback.
9. Keep everyone informed of new developments with frequent communications.
10. Encourage people to cooperate with each other to achieve customer satisfaction.
11. Make sure people are open to change when new challenges or strategies require it.
12. Give all people real input into decisions or changes which affect them.

Key Success Factor No. 3: Marketing

The famous management guru Peter Drucker once made this important statement about marketing, which all too few business leaders appreciate (emphasis mine):

"Because *the purpose of business is to create a customer*, the business enterprise has two– and only two– basic functions: marketing and innovation. Marketing and innovation produce results; all the rest are costs. Marketing is the distinguishing, unique function of the business."

Whether you call this success factor marketing, selling, customer relations or external communications, this, as I like to say, is *where the money comes from.* This is also the area where I have had the most personal experience, and I could write a book on this subject alone if space allowed. But instead I'm going to focus on the really, really important components we should all keep in mind and practice if we want to be successful.

Chances are, your business doesn't have a multi-million-dollar budget for ads during half-time of the Super Bowl or for direct mail to households across the country. Your marketing budget is probably limited, and you want to – need to – get the best bang for your buck.

There are plenty of websites and books which will give you thousands of small-to-midsize business marketing ideas and possibilities, but there are so many choices, it can be confusing to decide: Which approach is best for you? This chapter is designed to answer that question as concisely as possible.

Definition of marketing

First of all, we need to define what we are talking about.

Back in the 1950s, marketing was defined in terms of the "4 P's":

- **Product** (or service) which you provide for sale
- **Price,** which you charge for your product or service
- **Place** (or distribution), how and where you deliver your product or service to customers

- **Promotion**, how you communicate what your product/service has to offer, including advertising, public relations, personal selling, internet marketing and more.

(The "4 P's" are discussed in more detail in the later section about Managing Your Marketing Mix. Some industries add a 5th P, such as Packaging for the packaging industry, but the 4 P's are fairly universal.)

More recently, the American Marketing Association has defined marketing this way:

"Marketing is the activity, set of institutions, and processes for creating, communicating, delivering, and exchanging offerings that have value for customers, clients, partners, and society at large."

Got that? What this means is, importantly, marketing is not just something that a marketing person does. Marketing is a function of the whole organization or "set of institutions," or as we like to say in this book, a part of a living system.

Expanding on the AMA definition, first of all, you create value for customers in the form of products or services they want. Second, you communicate to these existing or potential customers that you have what they want. Third, you deliver the products or services to the paying customers. And long-term you manage relationships with customers in ways that benefit your organization and its stakeholders.

We also like this simple definition:

"Marketing involves orienting the business to meet the needs of the customer."

This is called the "marketing orientation" and has many benefits for any business. Again this stresses that it is a whole-organization function, with meeting the needs of the customer as its main focus. Now, how do we go about doing that?

The first constraint is, you've probably already decided what your business is. And your business is probably either what you like to do, what you want to do, or what your business is already doing. The problem with this is, maybe this is not what customers want to pay money for. The No. 1 reason that so many businesses fail, especially the newer ones, is that they do not offer products or services that enough people want to pay for!

Any town or city in America has seen restaurants, antique shops, clothing stores, consignment shops and many other retail establishments open their doors with high hopes, and close them before much time has passed, with huge debts and disappointments. It's a real heartache. The American dream becomes a nightmare. How can you keep that from happening to you? Instead of focusing mainly on what *you* want to do or what *you* like, focus on what *customers* need – and some of those needs are constantly changing, especially in the fast-paced 21st Century. As the saying goes, "Find a need and fill it."

Now let's turn to the 10 primary principles of the Marketing Success Factor:

1. Define your target markets in which you can sustain a competitive advantage.

You may not run the best pizza bakery in America, but you could provide the best pizza bakery within a one-mile radius of your store. Marketers often use the term "market segmentation" to mean define your target markets in segments such as location, demographics, values and more. The more specifically you can define your target markets, the better your chances of establishing a competitive advantage – something you naturally do better than your competition – that you can sustain over time. If someone wants a calamari pizza slathered in marinara sauce, you can be the dominator. A local lawyer in my market area focuses on serving bikers – he is a biker himself – and he promotes it constantly with TV advertising.

Don't try to be all things to all people! That is a prescription for disaster. Segment your markets in a way that you can dominate. In many ways marketing boils down to four words: "Market segmentation" and "product differentiation." This means your product (or service) is different from the competition in ways that appeal to your target market segments. Another little marketing axiom is, "Find a market small enough that you can dominate it." Don't aim for world domination until you find a way to be No. 1 in your neighborhood, area or city.

Sometimes a small part of a market segment is called a niche (pronounced "neesh"). Usually niche refers to a unique set of needs. For example, within the market segment of pizza buyers in your city, the small number of people who want to buy only Chicago-style pizzas or anchovy pizzas could be a niche. A niche is a specific portion of a market that shares a common interest or demographic. It may not be related to a common location or geography.

2. Continuously monitor customer needs, values and satisfaction.

Today's customers are a fickle bunch. They want to try out each new restaurant, then abandon it for the next one. They buy a product or service because all their friends are hyping it on social media, then when the fad fades, so does the business. Think of customer needs as a constantly moving wave and learn to ride the wave like an expert surfer – slightly ahead of the curve. Again this is something the average business never does, and suffers the consequences.

The ideal scenario is to find out what customers need and value *before* you start your business. This is highly recommended, for example, in developing a business plan as advocated by the Small Business Administration. But again almost no one does this. They launch a business based on what they like and assume other people will like it too. So let's assume your business is up and running, producing some kind of product or service, and you want to monitor customer needs, values and satisfaction. How would you do that? Here are some possibilities:

- **Hire a marketing consultant** or market research company to conduct an objective survey of your customers and, if possible, potential customers. Find out their perceptions, needs, values (what's important to them) and satisfaction with your business or other providers. This is the best approach if you can afford it. Hint: If you are a business-to-business company, a survey of even your top 10 customers can be very valuable if done objectively. My company did this for a number of clients on a low budget, and the results were actionable improvements in every case.

- **Contact a local college or university** that teaches marketing or business and see if there's a class that would like to work with you to do a survey for free. It gives you valuable objective results and gives them real-world market research experience.

- **Set up an online survey** using Survey Monkey, Google Forms or other free service. Email your customers (you do have your customers' emails, don't you?) and ask them to take the survey. Offer a drawing for a gift card or prize as a reward.

- **Mail a written survey** to customers or prospects for whom you have addresses. Include a self-addressed, stamped or business reply envelope. Again offer some prize or reward for participating.

- **Hand out a short survey** to customers visiting your store or place of business. Ask them to fill it out, fold it in half, and turn it in before they leave for a discount coupon good for any future purchase. We did this for a restaurant once and results were quite valuable, while the process was inexpensive.

- **Last is the old-fashioned approach** where the owner or manager walks around (again easy for a restaurant) and asks customers how their experience is going and what can you do better. Emphasize your interest in suggestions for improvement and not just a generic "Everything's fine" kind of answer. People may still tell you what they think you want to hear, but if you ask sincerely, you may get some valuable insights.

3. Build a unique brand positioning on a sustainable competitive advantage.

This is similar to our very first Principle under Strategy, and an example of how all five success factors are interrelated: "Focus on what you do best, a sustainable competitive advantage." If you do that, it is the job of marketing to build a unique brand positioning on this advantage. What does this mean?

"Positioning" refers to how your brand is going to be perceived in relation to your competition. In their highly regarded book, *Positioning: The Battle For Your Mind,* Al Ries and Jack Trout claimed that your mind perceives products in terms of hierarchies or ladders. Coca-Cola and Pepsi have battled for the top rung on the ladder of dark cola for many decades. The Ford Mustang competes with the Chevy Camaro. And so on through every business category.

So you have to stop and think, what category and particularly what hierarchy do you want to compete for? In simplest terms (real world is more complicated), companies compete on the bases of quality, price and service. There's a famous saying – "Quality, price, service. Pick two." This is because there are always trade-offs. Generally companies that offer top quality and excellent service charge a higher price. Think of Mercedes and BMW dealerships. Companies that try to be the low-cost provider often have to sacrifice some quality, some service or both. That's because excellent service requires your people to do more work for each customer purchase, and either you charge the customer extra for that or you give up profitability.

Keep in mind that whatever positioning you choose to promote through marketing, it must be realistic. If you claim to be the low-cost provider and stick the customer with high prices, you will ruin your reputation. If you claim to provide excellent service, you'd better constantly monitor your competition to see what sort of service they provide so you can stay one step ahead.

Recently I needed a major repair on my Toyota vehicle, and my local garage could not handle it. So I called the Toyota dealership where I had purchased my car, even though I knew I would pay full price because the new-car warranty had expired. This was in the time of the Coronavirus, yet I was surprised to learn that the dealer, located about 15 miles from my office, would drive to my location (with two drivers), pick up my car for the repair, and return it, all at no extra charge. I was assigned a customer service representative for the whole process. Even though the major repair cost me a lot of money, this was the best customer service I have ever experienced from an auto dealership and shows a real commitment to excellent, innovative service.

Somewhat surprisingly, the dealership does not promote this. They have the same old tired ads that say, "We have hundreds of cars to choose from and provide a lifetime warranty on all of them." It turns out that lifetime warranties are not provided by the manufacturer or dealer but by a third-party warranty company that the dealer contracts with, really a form of insurance. But that's another story.

Positioning strategy is best communicated with a short, memorable marketing slogan or positioning statement. Like "15 minutes could save you 15 percent or more on car insurance" from GEICO; "I'm lovin' it" from McDonalds, and "Always the low price. Always" from Walmart. This kind of positioning statement, stated creatively and repeated over and over, tends to sink into customers' minds and influence their perceptions of your business. But it must be believable if it is going to stick. (Not sure about McDonalds' slogan, which actually was created by a European advertising agency, although they have spent millions promoting it.)

For the small to mid-size business with limited marketing funds, the development of a brand can be an elusive goal. Ideally it can be the responsibility of everyone in the company through the use of memorable brand slogans and graphics that communicate clearly what the company stands for and how it differs from the competition. A good example is T-shirts with the company logo and brand statement, perhaps emphasized with a clever phrase, printed in bold visible type on the front and perhaps the back as well. Employees can wear them, and others can be given or sold to customers.

4. Attract new customers with targeted communications in multiple media.

Over the years I learned that in almost every case, industry leaders do more marketing communications than their competitors. Is all that marketing the cause of their top position or just something they can afford because they are the industry leader? Probably both.

Now if you have a small business with limited income, you are not going to be able to afford a lot of advertising. But anyone can afford to use free social media to reach out to potential customers and attract them to buy from you. Your message must speak to their needs and not just be "we're the best" chest-thumping. You can include promotions such as sale prices or limited-time availabilities. But there are many other options.

Here's a brief guide to marketing communications for your business:

1. **Manage your marketing mix** – For many years the marketing "mix" has been defined as a combination of the "4 P's" of marketing. These are the four primary variables of your marketing strategy and implementation:

(a) <u>Product</u> – the products or services you will offer to customers for sale. As noted above, you must select products or services that fill a real need, in a niche small enough that you can dominate it. But beyond just selecting your product or service, other important success factors must be carefully managed. Probably most important is quality. You need to offer products of high quality that the customer can depend on time and time again. The quality must be consistent and must conform to the customer's perceptions, not just yours. If you are in a service business – and even the act of selling products is a service – you must ensure that the whole customer experience is enjoyable. From the first point of contact with your business, through service delivery and the purchasing experience, and on to service or follow-up after the sale, every step needs to be carefully planned and managed (especially if you have employees) so the customer experiences pleasure and satisfaction at every step. Again regular honest feedback from your customers is vital to keep this customer experience not only positive but also continuously improving.

(b) <u>Price</u> – the price you will charge for your products or services. The customer not only pays money for your stuff – he or she also pays in time and effort. And the customer will consider all that when deciding to buy again. How much time or effort did the customer expend to obtain your offering? What can you do to minimize the time and effort so the purchase is exceptionally convenient and positive? Again think about the total experience and what you can do to continuously improve.

(c) <u>Place</u> – your place of business or how you deliver your products. Customers judge your business by your place of business or product distribution point even before they receive and use the product or service. Every little thing influences customer perceptions. In retail, not only is convenient location important, but also visibility from a main road, easy access in and out, and safety are all important factors in the consumer's mind (sometimes unconsciously) as he or she buys from you or considers buying. The way your employees are dressed, the interior furnishings and lighting, air conditioning, smell – all the senses are working to develop a perception of your business, product and service. Attention to detail is vital.

(d) <u>Promotion</u> – communications with potential and existing customers. This is the part of marketing that most people think IS marketing, but now you see it is only a fraction of it. "If you build it, they will come" might work for a "Field of Dreams," but it doesn't work for a business of reality in most cases. It is possible for a new store or restaurant in a well-located and high-traffic shopping center to attract customers with just some nice signage and an appealing storefront. But even this kind of business, like all others, can benefit from some well-planned, creative, and well-executed promotion.

Since this is so important (and what most people think marketing is), we'll devote the next whole section to it.

2. **Promoting your business** – there are over 50 different ways to promote your business through marketing communications, but generally they fall into a few major categories:

(a) <u>Advertising</u> is communication where you pay the media for carrying your message. Newspaper, radio and TV advertising can work well for businesses which sell to individuals and the public, but it can be fairly expensive. The famous New York merchant John Wannamaker is reported to have said, "50 percent of my advertising is a waste. I just don't know which 50 percent." Lots of small businesses that try various forms of advertising find that much of it seems to be a waste because there are no apparent sales resulting. One way to alleviate that common problem is to use some form of response tracking. You can make specific offers in different ads and ask customers to use the offer number when responding in order to get that particular deal. If you give coupons, of course, customers will need to bring them in to redeem them. With internet advertising a number of software programs allow you to track responses to your online ads and offers with great precision. Any way you cut it, advertising is expensive. You pay for media time and space. That's why I recommend that my customers take maximum advantage of "free" media time and space by using:

(b) <u>Public Relations</u>, also called PR or publicity. The catch here is that the news media will not run the same story repeatedly, as is the case with paid advertising. Instead, you must present something new – as the saying goes, "Three-fourths of NEWS is NEW." But even with a small business, there are often opportunities to get articles printed in local and sometimes national media about new products or services, new personnel or promotions, special events like seminars or open houses, and many other activities that skilled PR practitioners are good at. Most public relations firms have access to huge directories of practically all news media in the U.S. and abroad. These directories tell what each magazine or newspaper is interested in, its circulation, editors, contacts and much more. Often it is easier to get articles published in national trade magazines than local newspapers, depending on your industry and city.

One study found that public relations had *seven times the credibility* of advertising. Readers consider articles published by reputable media to be "facts," whereas advertising claims are often viewed with some skepticism.

(c) <u>Personal Selling</u> – This also is often considered to be the "same as" marketing, especially when practiced by full-time sales professionals. But there is a big difference. *Marketing* involves finding out what your *customers* want and giving it to them. *Selling* is deciding what *you* (or company owners) want to produce and trying to persuade customers to buy it. In the best organizations marketing helps create demand for needed products, making the sales job much easier and more user-friendly.

Personal selling is an art and a science. One book I highly recommend is called <u>*SPIN Selling* by Neil Rackham</u>. SPIN stands for Situation, Problem, Implication, Need, a four-step process uncovered by a team of experts observing expert salespeople at work. Fundamentally, the more you sincerely try to understand a potential customer's situation and develop an offering custom-tailored to his or her needs, the more likely you are to be successful. This consultative approach is also reflected in several other popular books on selling. And this is a very different approach from having a "script" where you talk and talk and talk at the potential customer until you wear down resistance and "close."

(d) <u>Internet Marketing</u> – Marketing via the Internet is a cross between public relations and advertising. You are paying for the media – your website – and you may pay for the content as well, by hiring a web design firm. But overall, the cost is much lower than print or broadcast advertising, and you can have thousands and thousands of words, depending on the richness of your site, with little or no extra cost. There is not sufficient space within this overall approach to the key success factors to go into all the intricacies of internet marketing success, which is constantly changing as the Internet landscape constantly evolves. But fundamentally a website is just some code on a computer in cyberspace – the trick is, getting potential customers to come to your site – generating traffic as it is called. Having lots of relevant content is a great way to make your site appealing to the search engines like Google and Bing. Keeping it constantly updated and refreshed enhances its appeal to search engines.

With all the hundreds of millions of websites online, with millions more being added all the time, getting free traffic requires what is called Search Engine Optimization (SEO). This means optimizing individual pages for certain keywords which potential customers are likely to enter into search engines. Of course you have to also file your website with search engines. Just enter the keywords "internet marketing" into a major search engine and you will find tons of information, some valuable and much of it designed to sell you an online e-book or series of CDs. But the more you know, the more effectively you can promote your business.

5. Develop customer relationships with strategic selling, database tracking systems, and caring.

Strategic selling involves managing a long-term relationship with each customer, including his or her present and future needs, instead of traditional selling which focuses on making the sale in the moment. Each person or company you sell to represents what is called a lifetime customer value. For example, a restaurant customer might only spend $20 for a meal once, but if you can get the customer to come back often, over a number of years, the total lifetime customer value could easily be in the thousands of dollars. Keeping in touch with each customer via an email newsletter or periodic updates helps sustain and enhance each long-term customer relationship.

You also need to try to capture each customer's name, email address and other contact information in a database, typically called a Customer Relationship Management (CRM) system. Some of these are available online for free. In addition to contact information, you can capture personal information such as family members, birthday, product or service preferences and more to help your business relate to each customer as a unique individual.

Caring for customers. The importance of caring for customers is aptly captured in the expression, "I don't care how much you know until I know how much you care." We are all human beings who want to feel other people love and care for us, and tapping into that need is one of the most powerful, if not the ultimate, customer relationship methods anyone can use. This doesn't mean erotic love for customers, of course, but it does mean that we need to convince our customers we really care about what's best for them, not just getting their money. How do we do that? A few keyways:

- Show an interest in customers as persons. Listen to them with empathy. Remember what they say. Record key information in a database so you and others don't forget.
- Give something extra. Provide a small product or service for free, as an expression of appreciation, not just at Christmas but unexpectedly, or give a special discount.
- Begin with a needs assessment. This is a powerful tool which some professionals use regularly but many other businesses can learn to do. This shows you really want to understand what your customers need and are not just trying to sell them something off the shelf or something that someone else bought. (Marketing is giving people what they want and need; selling is trying to persuade people to buy what you want to provide.)
- Remember to say "thank you." Don't take anyone's business for granted. Let them know you appreciate their business by explicitly telling them so.

6. Manage customer expectations and perceptions to ensure satisfaction.

Did you know that a customer's perceptions of the product or service provided by your company are shaped by their expectations, which you can manage before and after the sale? This led to the saying, "It is better to underpromise and overdeliver than to overpromise and underdeliver." Tell a customer that their job can be finished or their product delivered in two weeks, then provide it in one week, and you will have a happy customer. Tell the customer they can expect delivery in three days, then provide it in one week, and they will be disappointed.

Many people in business have "the need to please disease." This leads them to tell customers what they think they want to hear so they can get the sale, then deal with the dissatisfaction later on. It's often a case of short-term pleasure followed by long-term pain.

As Abe Lincoln famously said, "You can fool some of the people all of the time, and all of the people some of the time, but you can't fool all of the people all of the time." So as you seek to manage customer expectations and perceptions, honesty is the best policy. Decide what level of quality, price and service you can realistically sustain and tell customers what to expect. Then deliver exactly what you promised. Of course if a problem occurs like a delayed part over which you have no control, again keep the customer informed so that there is not a disappointing experience down the road.

7. Keep customers informed in language they understand.

Some services like haircuts and grocery checkout happen before your eyes, so you don't need the company to keep you informed during that time. But many other services and some product businesses do work that the customer cannot see but has to pay for. That's when it's especially valuable to keep customers informed in language they understand.

For example a custom chemical manufacturing company charges many thousands of dollars to make a certain chemical compound for its customers. The customer expects the output to meet its requirements exactly, on time and on budget. So it is vitally important that the chemical company provide the customer with regular updates in language they can understand – not chemical jargon.

Or consider a pharmacy refilling a prescription. Walgreens does an excellent job of keeping customers informed via text message and sometimes telephone when a prescription is being refilled, needs to be refilled, or there are any delays. If the information is too technical for a text message, they tell the customer to call their pharmacy for an explanation.

Many of us have had the experience of hiring a home repair or remodeling contractor, who starts the job with a flurry, then disappears, providing no explanation of why they did not continue. Sometimes the reason is a missing part, and sometimes the contractor is working multiple jobs at once and doesn't want the customer to know that. Whatever the reason, customers want to be kept informed in language they understand – no deception.

Most business processes work in three steps: input, throughput and output. The customer can see the input and output, but can be easily concerned about the throughput, especially if it takes more than a few hours. Just because the customer wants to know what is going on with their job doesn't mean they don't trust you – they are only human and have a need to know. Besides, they are the one paying the bill, so they deserve to know!

Practice continuous customer communications.

Customers' needs change from time to time, and you need a way to hear that clearly. In my experience most small businesses NEVER ask their customers, "How are we doing? What can we do to improve your satisfaction?" The reason for that, in many cases, is business leaders don't really want to know. If sales are up, they don't think they need to know. If sales are down, they don't want to hear bad news.

It does indeed take courage to ask customers about their satisfaction. But another obstacle is that customers will rarely tell their provider what they really think. If you survey your own customers, they are likely to tell you *what they think you want to hear*, not the real truth. The way around that is to use an objective professional research firm, and it can be much less expensive than you think.

Once we were doing a survey for a professional service client, and one of their customers was intrigued by our questions, including customer value and satisfaction. He told our interviewer, "You know, I realized in answering these questions that I would not say the same thing to my contact in that company. I can see there is real value in having an outside firm do this. Tell me how you come up with the questions, and what you do with the answers." And so we did.

For large financial or retail firms, where customer contact is frequent and the exchange relatively impersonal (buying a product, making a deposit etc.), Richard Whitely, author of *Customer-Centered Growth,* recommends what he calls "hardwiring the voice of the customer." This means that every single person who has customer contact is encouraged to capture comments, good or bad, and feed them into their central database. Some companies condense that information every day and feed it to key staff members in a concise report. Now *that* is continuous customer communication! The point is: Ask your customers what they want, listen to what they say, and act accordingly. This is one of the most powerful keys to success, so often ignored.

8. Encourage customer feedback and communicate it internally to all concerned.

Big companies like Amazon and other online retailers automatically send "how did we do" emails to customers as soon as the product is delivered. Now the situation is reversed from No. 7 above and instead of the customer needing to know what they can't observe, the company needs to know what they can't observe. They have computerized reports stating the product was delivered, but were you the customer satisfied? Did it arrive in good condition in the right place as you specified? Do you have any questions or feedback you want to provide?

For big companies, this kind of data is a part of their internal business processes. The information is gathered electronically and distributed to everyone involved so they can "keep score" and strive for continuous improvement.

Even a small business like a hotel or restaurant can provide customers with feedback cards to share their experiences. Or at least once a year ask customers to fill out a short online survey (keep it under 5 minutes for best results) so you have some objective feedback to guide your operations and strategy.

9. Ensure customer enthusiasm with a proprietary interaction process.

Most people have never experienced a proprietary interaction process or even know what the term means.

If you have ever stayed at a Ritz-Carlton Hotel, you know. Ritz-Carlton is famous for bending over backwards to satisfy customers, even at their own expense. Each employee is empowered to spend up to $2,000 to satisfy each customer. For example, one customer got home and discovered they had left their laptop charger in their room. By the time they contacted the hotel, they discovered that Ritz-Carlton had already sent them the charger overnight via FedEx.

Zappos, the online shoe retailer, is known for accepting customer returns, no questions asked, even if the customer has used or abused the shoes.

And Nordstrom also empowers all its personnel to go the extra mile to take care of customers. One time, a Nordstrom employee noticed that a customer left their luggage and flight itinerary in the parking lot of the store. The employee got into their own car and drove the customer's luggage to the airport and found her before her flight took off.

In all of these cases, customers are wowed by the extraordinary service and become quite loyal as a result. As noted previously, consider the lifetime value of each customer and not just the income from one transaction. Ritz-Carlton sets what it calls the "Gold Standard" for proprietary interaction processes as it provides each employee with its statement of 12 Service Values. This is such an excellent example for any business to follow, we reproduce the 12 Values here:

1. I build strong relationships and create Ritz-Carlton guests for life.
2. I am always responsive to the expressed and unexpressed wishes and needs of our guests.
3. I am empowered to create unique, memorable and personal experiences for our guests.
4. I understand my role in achieving the Key Success Factors, embracing Community Footprints and creating The Ritz-Carlton Mystique.
5. I continuously seek opportunities to innovate and improve The Ritz-Carlton experience.
6. I own and immediately resolve guest problems.
7. I create a work environment of teamwork and lateral service so that the needs of our guests and each other are met.
8. I have the opportunity to continuously learn and grow.
9. I am involved in the planning of the work that affects me.
10. I am proud of my professional appearance, language and behavior.
11. I protect the privacy and security of our guests, my fellow employees and the company's confidential information and assets.
12. I am responsible for uncompromising levels of cleanliness and creating a safe and accident-free environment.

What can your business do to develop and maintain a proprietary interaction process? Think about it. Every contact with a customer including the first phone call or email is an opportunity to make an impression that "we are different, and we really care about our customers." But all team members must be trained in this process if it is to be maintained and believable.

Another way to enhance customer enthusiasm is through:

One-To-One Marketing

This phrase, popularized by Don Peppers and Martha Rogers' book, *The One To One Future*, is based on an approach many marketers have learned through experience. The way I like to express this is, "The unit of marketing is the relationship between two individual people." What this means is, people want to be treated and known as individuals.

The best way to facilitate this is with a computer database which keeps track of each customer or prospect's contact information, characteristics and preferences. Some Customer Relationship Management (CRM) software will pull up a customer's key information file automatically when caller ID identifies their incoming phone call. If that doesn't work, their name or phone number manually entered will pull it up. But on an even more personal basis, have one person assigned as THE contact person for each customer.

For large-potential sales, encourage your personnel to build personal relationships with key customers. Find out about their likes, hobbies, families and more, and capture it in a protected database. Correctly used, computers can *increase* customer intimacy and loyalty. But only when that company-customer contact is experienced as one-to-one, person-to-person, and not generic or impersonal "customer support."

10. Monitor competitor moves and market trends to be proactively prepared.

Earlier we spoke of how living systems in the natural world constantly adapt to the changing environment so they can survive and thrive. The same applies to businesses.

In his massive PIMS study (which stands for Profit Impact of Market Strategy), Bradley Gale discovered that customer buying choices are always *relative to the perceived value offered by competitors*. So you may be thinking your customers are loyal and will always buy from you, then along comes a competitor offering superior value (basically a desirable combination of quality, price and service), and suddenly your income drops. Walmart destroyed thousands of small-town businesses by offering local residents products of equal or better quality at much lower prices.

If you run a retail business and a competitor moves into your neighborhood, shop them like a customer would to experience what they have to offer. No matter what kind of business you have, you can "shop the competition" by doing an online search for terms that combine your business category and market area, such as "insurance agency Omaha" or "auto repair Miami." Check out their websites and be sure your site is competitive. And if possible shop the competitors by buying their products or services or at least meeting with them for a quote. If you are afraid of revealing your identity, hire a "mystery shopper" through a local service or hire a part-timer for the purpose.

Market trends can be monitored online as well. Many industry sectors have free email newsletters to track trends. You might benefit from joining a trade association for your business category and attending seminars on the latest trends. Or hire a service or freelancer to track trends for you and provide you with reports.

A free alternative is to set up a Google alert to monitor any search term of your choosing and deliver results to you via email on a regular basis.

Don't keep your head in the sand or your nose on the grindstone. Look around and see what is going on in the marketplace. Adapt quickly to stay ahead of the competition, survive and thrive.

Interrelationships with Other Success Factors

Finally, as a checklist for ensuring effective 21st-Century **marketing**, consider its interrelationships with the other Key Success Factors with questions like these:

- Has our **strategy** been created with objective research into the needs and perceptions of customers, and is it constantly updated as customer needs evolve and change?

- Do our **people** throughout the organization understand our marketing program, and do they fully support it in day-to-day interaction with customers, as well as informal contacts with friends and family in the community?

- Is our marketing congruent with our **operations**, so that operations deliver what marketing promises on a consistent basis?

- Is marketing closely integrated with our **finances**, so that we have specific goals for sales and income, and so that marketing gets the financial support it needs for advertising, public relations, personal selling, internet marketing and other forms of outreach?

Key Success Factor No. 3: Marketing – Chapter Summary

1. Define your target markets in which you can sustain a competitive advantage.
2. Continuously monitor customer needs, values and satisfaction.
3. Build a unique brand positioning on a sustainable competitive advantage.
4. Attract new customers with targeted communications in multiple media.
5. Gain new customers with strategic selling and database tracking systems.
6. Manage customer expectations and perceptions to ensure satisfaction.
7. Keep Customers Informed in Language They Understand
8. Encourage customer feedback and communicate it internally to all concerned.
9. Ensure customer enthusiasm with a proprietary interaction process.
10. Monitor competitor moves and market trends to be proactively prepared.

Key Success Factor No. 4: Operations

Operations are the core of the business. This is how the people in the business create value for customers, which drives sales and income, which keeps the business alive. Nothing is more important, but because operations tend to become daily habits, doing the same thing day after day, they are often taken for granted and are quite difficult to change. Here are the seven key success factors for operations.

1. Align and fine-tune operations to deliver superior customer value.

The successful company is customer-driven, understands what customers value most, and aligns its operations to deliver superior customer value with dependability and excellence.

Many companies start out delivering the products or services that the owners or leaders like. Someone loves collecting antiques, so she opens an antique store. Someone likes cooking seafood, so he opens a seafood restaurant. While it is important for the key people in the organization to enjoy what they are doing, business is all about meeting customer needs, specifically what customers value most.

For example a McDonalds restaurant is geared for low cost and speed. McDonalds' customers do not expect a gourmet restaurant experience. They value low cost and fast service, so they go to McDonalds and other fast-food restaurants to get it. McDonalds' operations are documented with detailed operations manuals so that every customer gets what he or she values every time.

Superior customer value can only be determined by asking customers what they value most. In the early days of a business, this might involve the owner or other manager informally asking customers what is important to them and were they satisfied with their purchase. As soon as the company has a little revenue, or perhaps using start-up funds, a professional market research study should be conducted to ask customers *objectively* what they value most in a supplier of *x* (the product or service category you operate in), how important each criterion is to them, and how the company ranks on those criteria.

As explained in the previous section on Managing Customer Value, this generates a customer value profile that shows Value A has an importance of A%, and the company ranks X on a scale of 1 to 10; Value B has an importance of B%, and the company ranks Y on a scale of 1 to 10, and so on through all the significant values. This kind of information is tremendously valuable if used properly. Even calling 10-12 customers randomly can be very illuminating when a consensus emerges, although slight differences cannot be considered statistically significant.

In his excellent book *Managing Customer Value* mentioned earlier, Bradley Gale suggests going the next step and analyzing which departments are responsible for producing those individual items customers value most. You can create a matrix-type chart to illustrate this. Then an action plan can be developed to improve customer value creation on a department-by-department or person-by-person basis. This must be put in writing, on paper or on electronic files which can be accessed over the Internet or internal computer network.

If you want to improve your operations, build a system to guarantee delivery of *the value which customers want*. If your customers want quality, build a system that checks quality at every key step, not just at the end. If your customers want speed, study ways to cut out time-wasting steps and replace them with consolidated simpler ones, perhaps using computer systems to make things move faster.

The key point here is, don't just look at your operations and ask yourself, "How can we improve this?" Start instead with what customers value most, step back from day-to-day habits, and try to design an ideal system for delivering that value consistently.

2. Document, measure and control operations with full employee input.

Quality-oriented companies pursue TQM (Total Quality Management) or ISO (International Standards Organization) certification by writing down detailed operating procedures. Organizations like major fast-food companies and hotel chains have very detailed operations manuals for everything from fixing food to cleaning bathrooms. Nothing is left to chance.

But any company no matter how small can simply start by asking its people to write down what they do step by step, then using that as a basis to develop a comprehensive operations manual and drive continuous improvements. Of course, just because someone writes down a series of steps does not mean this is the best way to do the job, but it is an excellent starting point that gets team members involved form the beginning. This first draft then needs to be reviewed by knowledgeable personnel, be they managers or line staff, to see what improvements can be made. Going forward, the documents can and should be reviewed periodically so that they reflect current practices and any improvements which arise naturally.

3. Explain operations so that people understand their responsibilities for creating value.

It is vital that each employee who is responsible for implementing any part of the operations manual fully understand what is expected and has a positive attitude toward doing so. If each person feels he or she "owns" that section of the manual in terms of responsibility and pride, following the steps is more likely to occur.

Don't come down from the mountain like Moses with your new Ten Commandments. Let all your people get involved in analyzing and designing how operations can be improved to deliver greater customer value.

It never ceases to amaze me how "ordinary people" can come up with great insights for improving operations. One manufacturer we worked with told the story of how a janitor cleaning the production floor noticed that a big machine was not working right and suggested an improvement that saved the company thousands of dollars. Your workers are often the ones closest to the action, or the ones who hear any customer complaints. Involving your people will not only yield a much greater abundance of good ideas, it will also greatly strengthen the likelihood that improvements will happen.

Try to ensure that every team member understands what customers value, how the company creates that value, and how they are responsible for contributing to that process as best they can.

If you have a big company and it's not practical to involve everyone in the whole improvement process, then organize what John Kotter calls a "guiding coalition." This is not just the top people but a cross-section involving all levels. Be politically shrewd and include people who have a lot of personal power and influence at lower levels even if they are not managers. Consider involving even your chronic rebels. They often have a lot of energy and strength, and by being involved in the improvement process, they will come to support it and advocate it with others.

4. Encourage innovation and collaboration throughout the organization.

Continuous improvement in operations is just one of many ways a company can innovate. Someone may come up with an idea for a new product or service that has never been offered before but would be a good fit for the company's range of services.

Larger companies can have teams dedicated to research and development of new products. Smaller ones can have occasional brainstorming sessions on-site or off to a surge of innovative ideas.

Frequent customer research, asking customers what they want and what improvements they would like to see, can further stimulate innovation.

Reading trade journals, websites or emails can keep interested people apprised of new developments in their field and what competitors are up to.

Everyone in the company should be encouraged to come up with innovative ideas and rewarded in some fashion such as money, perks, or recognition in group events.

In addition to innovation, collaboration is also vital for peak performance. Sometimes the invisible lines between departments might as well be brick walls in terms of limiting collaboration, and some old-style companies even discourage people "getting out of their lanes." But the most successful companies take a holistic approach and encourage collaboration. "We're all in this together."

For example, conflicts between sales and operations occur in many companies. Salespeople want to tell customers "Sure, we can do that" to get the sale, but sometimes they have no idea how the promised product or service can be provided as desired. Operations people can also be off in their own world making stuff with little or no customer contact. They become reluctant to try anything new for fear of failure of discomfort. Management has to intervene in situations like this and encourage full collaboration with the goal of providing superior customer value at all times.

One way to increase collaboration is through cross-functional teams. Special teams can be formed including representatives from sales and marketing, operations, finance, personnel, management and more, so that each team is like the whole business in miniature. Or cross-functional teams can be more limited, combining only sales and operations for example, depending on the size of the staff and critical issues which need to be addressed.

But operations improvements cannot be entirely delegated to teams or a committee (unless you lead it) or left to a consultant's intervention. You as the manager-leader model the corporate culture of those who report to you. So you must have a passion for operations improvement in your gut, or it will not happen.

Essentially, changing any organization requires a *new energy force* moving in a direction different from business as usual. You might conjure up that energy within you just by thinking about how messed up your operations are. Or maybe you get the results from a customer survey that show distinct dissatisfaction. All too often it takes a crisis like a big drop in income or the loss of a major client to shake an organization into a state of readiness for operations improvement.

In his excellent book *Leading Change*, John Kotter advocates that you stimulate energy by *creating a sense of urgency*. Maybe there is indeed a crisis. Or maybe you "engineer" one to make your point. However you get the energy going, however many people you involve, you the manager-leader have to drive the improvement process.

5. Change or correct operations when something goes wrong so it won't repeat.

Sounds simple, but so often this does not happen. Earlier in this book we talked about the value of having a Learning Organization, which learns from mistakes and changes operations so those mistakes don't happen again.

Corrective actions only endure if the organization has standard procedures as noted above, in print or online, that people are expected to follow. If a standard procedure causes the failure, it needs to be updated and everyone involved needs to be informed. Often a failure is a learning opportunity – something that is not written down occurs or goes wrong – and then the standard procedures can be expanded and improved.

A mistake can cost any company thousands of dollars, especially if you lose all the business of a major customer (think lifetime customer value). So don't just improve in the moment – improve for the long haul so that this mistake won't happen again, and you benefit as a result.

It is possible if you disappoint or anger an existing customer, you can get them back again by sincerely apologizing to them in person, explaining what steps have been taken to correct the problem so it won't happen again, offer them some compensation for any damages or harm your company has caused, and ask them to give you another chance. The bigger the customer, the more important this "please forgive" process is conducted by the CEO or owner, whose commitment means the whole company is committed to making that customer feel satisfied and regaining loyalty.

Some companies have found a comprehensive measurement system like *The Balanced Scorecard* can be a great way to measure performance of all the key success factors. Others try to measure too many things and get bogged down in minutiae. One financial company actually expected managers to monitor and be judged based on over 200 measurement points! So the trick is to pick just a few key indicators of improvement, measure them continuously, and share the results.

All operations can benefit from computer information systems and programs that monitor performance and provide instant feedback. But remember the KISS rule – "Keep It Short and Simple" for best results with most team members.

I like the analogy of driving a car with simple measurements such as the speedometer, odometer, gas gauge, and warning lights. In fact some people use the term "dashboard" to refer to the ideal small set of measurements that help people stay on course. (Contrast that with the controls of a 747 jet, which require a crew of people to monitor and control.) For example:

- If you want to improve quality, count mistakes as well as fault-free results.
- If you want to improve speed, track cycle time, how long it takes your people to complete a defined task.
- If you want to improve customer satisfaction and retention, track complaints, or better yet do a frequent short customer survey that is meaningful enough to allow specific feedback, not just a generic restaurant-type card. Be sure to seek information on changing customer needs and preferences or this year's solution will be obsolete next year.

It is amazing how just the simple act of measuring a performance indicator and posting the results with either a wall chart or on your internal computer network can motivate people to do better, especially if there is a clear link between their own performance and one or more indicators. In fact it is very important for people to understand that linkage. Ideally individual performance is also measured and rewarded in terms consistent with your corporate measurement system.

6. Continuously improve operations with enthusiastic participation.

It's one thing to make a correction when something goes wrong. It's another thing for your people to embrace continuous improvement with enthusiasm.

Many Japanese companies practice what is known as *kaizen*, which means "continuous improvement." They have learned that over time, dozens or hundreds of small improvements suggested by team members can add up to huge gains in productivity and profitability.

Some companies boost enthusiastic participation by recognizing through formal awards ceremonies the employees who make the most useful suggestions. You can do the same on a scale and method which works best for your business.

Although financial incentives may seem the obvious reward, studies have shown that group recognition is even more powerful. Of course if someone's suggestion for improvement saves the company thousands of dollars or generates more in new income, it would only be fair to share the wealth with the person whose idea was the driver of the profitable improvement.

7. Strengthen operations with effective computer information systems and programs

Today the world's largest companies practically all use advanced computer systems to keep every employee on track and connected, with virtually every staff member having access to a centralized database and relevant software. But that is not the case for the many thousands of small to mid-size companies that employ a substantial portion of the nation's and world's workforce.

The problem is often that off-the-shelf software is too generic to adequately capture the company's business processes, but custom-coded software is too expensive.

We once worked with a small group of restaurants that had standard POS (point of sale) software driving their cash registers, but no way to make sure each employee was following standard procedures for his or her job. For example each dish served was made according to a recipe, but once a cook or other back-of-house staffer memorized the recipe, they went about fixing that dish the way they remembered, sometimes improvising and sometimes leaving out one or more key ingredients. There were standard procedures necessary to open the restaurant each morning and prepare of the day, and for securely closing the restaurant at the end of each evening, not leaving a mess behind.

So the affordable solution we improvised was to create an online operations manual consisting of standard Word documents and Excel spreadsheets, listing step by step what was to be done for each part of the business. These documents could be accessed by any restaurant manager, and they were updated from time to time as needed for changes and improvements. They were also printed and bound in 3-ring notebooks so anyone on staff could quickly access the needed information for any particular job or task.

Low-tech? Yes. Affordable and practical? Yes. Because following standard procedures is so essential for quality and customer satisfaction, any up-to-date information system is better than none. So don't let the cost of custom software stop you from standardizing operations. KISS (Keep It Short and Simple) and get 'er done rather than wishing for the ideal and never getting it.

For many years I ran my business using a customized relational database that allowed me to produce practically any kind of form, plan or document my business needed. It was essential for our success. But it took me untold hours to create it, and access by other team members was limited on a module basis, such as our new business development module. Nevertheless, it can be done if you or someone else on staff has the motivation and time to do it. Push through and the financial and operational rewards are substantial.

8. Manage operations to produce the customer-valued balance of quality, price, service and speed.

Earlier we talked about *Managing Customer Value* and how to create a customer value profile representing what your customers want and in what priority. Great concept, but you have to actually *deliver* what customers want, what they value most. So operations has to step up to the plate and deliver what research shows that *customers* want, not primarily what the *company* or *owners* want. And that requires a lot of discipline and realism.

Now if you do or outsource an authentic market research study of customer value, you will find that customers answer in their own words, and you have to decide whether to translate that into your own words or leave it in their words. Translation is necessary to aggregate the answers and translate them into action, but customer words can provide granular detail that should not be lost for best results. It's a judgment call, and that's why it's worth hiring an expert to help you.

For example, instead of

- …Quality, the customer may say, "I want something to last."
- …Price, the customer may say, "Affordable."
- …Service, the customer may say, "Treat me with respect."
- …Speed, the customer may say, "Don't make me wait too long."

And then there are trade-offs. Perhaps you have seen the sign or T-shirt that says, "Quality, Price, Speed. Pick two." Do you get the point? If you want a low price and fast service, you may have to sacrifice quality. If you want high quality and high speed, you are going to have to pay a high price. And so on.

The problem is made worse by today's consumer expectations set by giant companies like Amazon.

- Search for a product on amazon.com.
- Find product at a great price.
- Click the "buy" button.
- Place your order.
- Boom – it is at your front door in 24-48 hours, sometimes less.

Why can't everything be that easy, right? You got quality, price and speed all combined. So how is a small business going to compete?

You're going to compete on customized service. Remember that is your competitive advantage when competing with the big guys in almost every case.

Amazon can sell you standard food items, but it is not going to sell you a complete meal, freshly cooked just the way you want, or refill your wine glass or coffee cup whenever it starts to get low.

Amazon can sell you all kinds of jewelry, but it is not going to gift wrap it with beautiful paper and a ribbon bow and place it in your hands at the moment of purchase.

To compete with Amazon or any other company, try to understand exactly what your customers want and deliver it to them with customized service that no one else can match. There will always be demand for that, and usually a willingness to pay extra for it too.

Control products and services differently.

If you are a manufacturer, controlling operations by measuring physical products is fairly straightforward compared with measuring services. Most books on quality, operations or business process improvement are written from the manufacturing perspective. If you're in the service business, don't think these books are going to do you much good. A few determined service businesses have indeed been successful with TQM or ISO9000, and my hat's off to them. But the amount of time wasted by service businesses (including mine) trying to adopt manufacturing-based operations methodology is staggering.

One of the best, classic books on service quality is *Delivering Service Quality* by Valarie Zeithaml et al. This research/authoring team was the first to define service quality as a matter of "balancing customer perceptions and expectations." Since then there have been a bunch of books on the subject, as you'll see if you type "service quality" into the search window at amazon.com. Service quality essentially:

- Is a matter of customer perceptions; for customers *perception is reality*.
- Can be influenced by carefully *managing customer expectations*.
- Is *individualized for every company*, based on their customer relationships, skills, history, community, competitors and many other factors. So you have to chart your own path, but ask your customers which direction to follow.

Interrelationships with Other Success Factors

Finally, as a checklist for ensuring effective 21st-Century **operations**, consider its interrelationships with the other Key Success Factors with questions like these:

- Do our operations reflect our overall **strategy** for the future, or are they more set in the status quo?

- Have our operations been defined and improved with the full involvement of our **people**, and do they reflect what they care about and are committed to?
- Do our operations reflect the needs of our **markets**, as determined by objective research or surveys into the needs, perceptions and preferences of customers, prospects, and others outside of the organization?
- Have we considered the **financial** aspects of our operations, how we are going to pay for planned improvements, how operations can increase income and profits, and how operations can help ensure the continuing financial strength of the organization?

Key Success Factor No. 4: Operations – Chapter Summary

1. Operations are aligned and fine-tuned to deliver superior customer value.
2. Operations are documented, measured and controlled with full worker input.
3. Operations are explained so that people understand responsibilities for creating value.
4. Encourage innovation and collaboration throughout the organization.
5. Operations are changed or corrected when something goes wrong so it won't repeat.
6. Operations are continuously improved with enthusiastic participation.
7. Operations are aided by effective computer information systems and programs.
8. Operations produce the customer-valued balance of quality, price, service and speed.

Key Success Factor No. 5: Finances

Finances is the short name for this success factor, but it also includes **facilities and equipment**, since owned facilities and equipment are both financial investments and financial assets, and rented facilities and equipment are a major expense.

We don't claim to be financial advisors, but we've managed our own company's finances for over 35 years and worked with a number of client companies with financial issues. However, many small businesses including ours need the help of an accounting or CPA firm to guide wise financial management, even with an internal bookkeeper. So don't feel obligated to do all this on your own; get professional help as needed. Here are 10 important principles in the Finances success factor:

1. Plan for the capital and cash flow you need to be successful.

If you are planning or starting a new business, it is extremely important to plan for the money you will need to get your business running and keep it operating until you have sufficient income to support operations. If your business is already generating adequate income, you will likely need additional money, often in the form of a loan, to buy new equipment or expand. All too many small to mid-size businesses fail because they run out of money. Don't let that happen to you.

The Small Business Administration website SBA.gov has excellent resources about planning and managing your business finances, including various sources of funding. All of this information is free and well developed, so take the time to read it and absorb it.

Some businesses such as marketing and web design firms, as well as other small service businesses, have virtually no start-up costs except for computers and Internet access, which just about everyone reading this has already. Such entrepreneurs can usually work from home until they can afford office space – and some continue to work from home indefinitely. I know a highly successful importer of furniture, selling for millions of dollars a year to major retailers like Target, who has a team of eight people all over the world, all working from home. Increasingly, due in part to changes in workstyle driven by the Coronavirus pandemic, companies of all sizes are WFH (working from home) and saving a ton of money on rent and utilities as a result.

However, if your heart is set on starting a coffee shop, restaurant, print shop, construction company or other equipment-dependent business, you will need lots of capital to start, to continue and to expand.

If you need more money than you have, check out the funding sources on SBA.gov and give a call to your local Chamber of Commerce for other possibilities. For many businesses, getting start-up capital can be a tremendous challenge. Just because you have a desire or dream to start a capital-intensive business does not mean the money will miraculously appear. Lenders, whether personal or institutional, need to believe that they will get their money back, usually with interest. They not only have to believe in you – they also have to believe your business concept is viable and that you can pull it off.

You should also plan to invest your own money, either with cash or collateral on your assets, such as a second mortgage on your home. This demonstrates to other potential lenders that you believe so strongly in your business concept, you are willing to take serious personal risk.

Other potential sources include family and friends, banks and credit unions (loans and lines of credit), venture capitalists, angel investors, small business incubators, government grants, crowdfunding and credit cards.

It may take a great deal of time, research and effort to get sufficient funding if your new or growing business requires large sums of capital to get off the ground or grow. Try to find someone like a local banker or a relative in business who will shoot straight with you in terms of the viability of your concept and the likelihood of getting OPM (Other People's Money).

Remember: it's not just having enough money to buy the equipment and hardware you need, it's having the cash flow to pay your bills, most especially your payroll on a timely basis. Don't trust fortune, luck or God to bail you out. Be a responsible steward of money, plan carefully and spend cautiously.

Here are a few other tips about the importance and techniques of managing cash flow:

1. Cash flow is king. It doesn't matter much how much your company, product or service *could* make. What matters, your lifeblood, is, do you have the cash today to pay your bills? The main reason so many dot-coms became dot-bombs is they used their cash (from investors) so fast they called it (and still do) "burn rate." That's like living at home and having your parents pay all the bills – not the real world.

To succeed in business or other endeavors, you have to watch your cash flow very carefully. Accrual accounting is great for forecasting your success, but it does not reflect cash in the bank, so you need to watch both to know where your business stands. In fact, if you are a top company officer, you should watch your cash flow so carefully that you have an intuitive feel for it. That way if something goes wrong (like embezzling or a sudden income drop) you can sense the problem and check it out.

2. Cash flow is always cyclical. I have never seen a business yet that did not have ebbs and flows in cash volume. The cycle may be annual or multi-year, but those who've been around a while learn that there's a real law of nature -- "to everything there is a season, a time to reap and a time to sow." When your cash flow is strong, it is so tempting to spend it and so wise to save some. Financial conservatism always pays big dividends.

I remember years ago talking to an old entrepreneur who had turned a small business into a major manufacturer of boots for the Army and was a multimillionaire. He seemed to be just a basic "good old boy," as they say in the South. I asked him, in effect, how did he get to be so rich? And I'll never forget his answer: "By not spending money." He manufactured Army boots in a former school building out in the country, which he no doubt acquired very cheaply.

Before you sign that lease for the expensive office or buy all that new furniture, be sure there will be ample cash in the bank to cover essentials like payroll in the inevitable slow times. That way you will be more likely to survive much longer.

3. You cannot save yourself out of a hole. I've seen many companies hit hard times and try to cut, cut, cut to get out of the hole. Cutting expenses can help, but it almost never helps as much as increasing sales. Severe cutting tends to make the patient bleed to death. Morale hits bottom and instills a negative mindset.

Instead, adopt what is called "an abundance mentality." There is a ton of business out there, and if you've followed our other Success Factor tips, you know how to target your markets, sharpen your advantage and go for it. Keep your spirits up and go cheerfully after new business. Price your products/services aggressively and "optionally" (as noted earlier). Be a joy to work with. "The Lord helps those who help themselves." Self-mutilation is not the way out of the hole.

2. Maintain competitive pricing to ensure customer value.

In some market sectors such as luxury automobiles, high prices may be advantageous in signaling to the buyer that the product is truly superior and worth the higher price. But in general it is important to keep your pricing on par with what your competitors are charging. If competitor pricing is not readily available, such as on their websites, you might need to hire a "mystery shopper" to contact competitors for quotes. Of course if you can offer equal or superior quality at a lower price, that can be a competitive advantage. Always keep in mind:

The customer never buys a product or service. The customer buys value. That is a paraphrase of Bradley Gale's great book, *Managing Customer Value*, which we've mentioned before. If you want to increase sales and profits, give the customer more value. How do you do that? You begin with a customer survey (or better yet use a professional survey firm to help). Find out exactly what the customer values when selecting a supplier like your firm. Don't guess—it's a lot more complicated than top quality at lowest price with great service. Other factors such as fast turn-around, innovation and image (Mercedes, Apple, Polo etc.) are also important in many sectors.

One of the best ways to offer more value than your competitors, to justify an equal or higher price, is to provide more information. Don't just give an ordinary product or service. Give the customer extra information about how to use what you sell to enhance their business or life. Help the customer avoid traps. Go beyond the Golden Rule to the Platinum Rule: Do unto others as *they* would have you do unto them. The added value you offer may not mean added costs for either party, but it sure can mean added customer satisfaction, retention, or that popular phrase, "customer delight."

3. Use sophisticated financial controls to monitor cash flow and ensure profits.

Many entrepreneurs manage their finances with their checkbook, as they do their own personal finances, but this is not best practice for small to midsize businesses. It is better to have a complete accounting software program operated by a trained bookkeeper or accountant to make sure your cash flow is adequately strong and that you are actually making profits every month. Even if you have sales and income, that does not mean your income exceeds expenses, yielding a profit. And some items like capital equipment may be expensed differently from routine expenses such as office supplies. Again a skilled bookkeeper or accountant can help you monitor and analyze this with reporting at least once a month.

4. Take time to understand and track key financial data regularly.

It won't do you any good if you leave accounting to the accountants. Cash flow problems are one of the main reason small businesses fail. And unfortunately all too many small businesses have suffered embezzlement by an internal financial person they trusted. While not a common problem, it is always a danger, and I have had several close friends who lost many thousands due to an embezzling employee. So you must understand what your business number mean, keep an eye on them, and be alert when something doesn't look right.

At least once a week get a timely "snapshot" financial report from your accountant or bookkeeper such as accounts receivable (who owes you money) and accounts payable (who you owe money to). Once a month you need an updated income statement showing whether or not you had a net profit for the month, and a financial statement showing total liabilities, assets and other big-picture items. If you have no financial management experience, get your financial person to explain what the numbers mean, learn about them online, or buy and read a well-rated book. Basic financial expertise and number-tracking is essential for business success.

5. Use modular and flexible pricing so customers have choices.

I'll never forget a favorite client telling me, "Don't show me just one suit on the rack and expect me to buy." Now I wasn't selling men's clothing, but his statement applies to any product or service category. Most customers want options so they can make informed choices and feel in control.

For any proposal to a potential or existing customer, consider offering price points that are low, medium and high, and explain the differences. Also if you have a high-dollar project you're competing on, consider breaking it down into sections or modules with individual pricing for each. For example, we've often found it helpful with large projects which are hard to quote upfront due to lack of details, to instead start with a low-budget analysis-planning process whereby you work with the client to flesh out the details, then your estimate will be more precise, and the project will go more smoothly. The client can benefit from the analysis and planning even if they decide not to accept your recommendations, but in most cases they will, and you have a new client with a running start.

6. Know the real costs of products and services so real profits are achieved.

Unfortunately, just knowing your overall monthly profits is not sufficient to know which products or services were actually money losers or money gainers. Breaking all services down to specific projects allows more accurate tracking of income vs. expenses for each project. Detailed tracking of product costs and sales is also very worthwhile. Typically 80% of the profits in a business come from 20% of the products/services, so it's very important to know what parts of your business you want to expand and what you might cut or stop offering.

7. Be sure each employee understands how his or her performance impacts profits.

In some organizations employees have an overt or covert "us versus them" attitude toward management which can lead to behaviors which are unprofitable or worse. At the opposite end of the spectrum is the open book approach whereby management shares virtually all financial details with employees so they fully understand. A moderate approach would involve first analyzing how each employee's performance does impact profits, then explaining that to each one. On top of that add some kind of reward or incentive for contributing to profitable sales or operations, and the results can be dramatic. Sharing this information in some form with each employee helps them feel included and part of the team, while enhancing their professional development and learning.

8. Align financial rewards with results – not just longevity.

As noted above, when individuals, teams and the company as a whole are rewarded based on actual financial results, the right behaviors are reinforced and tend to be repeated. Giving people annual raises regardless of performance does not reinforce behaviors that are financially beneficial for the company, and may have the opposite effect. Let people know early on that annual raises are not automatic – and the only valid source of raises is increased profits, which they must help generate. This is a corollary to Principle 7 above.

9. Retain sufficient earnings to balance out economic cycles.

If the company spends all its profits as they come in, or passes them on to company owners such as with an S Corp., there's nothing left in the company when down times come. For many reasons the economy goes through up and down cycles over the years. The famous financier J. P. Morgan, when asked what the market will do, is quoted as replying, "It will fluctuate." If the economy is up now, you can be sure that a down cycle will follow in the not-too-distant future. A good practice is for company owners or shareholders to draw out just the money they need to live on, and save the rest. Ideally put some in an interest-bearing financial instrument or investment portfolio and not just leave it in the bank, given historically low interest rates.

10. Provide adequate facilities and equipment for the work to be done.

Worn-out, shoddy or out-of-date facilities and equipment tend to lower morale and productivity. They can also make a poor impression on customers or prospects who visit your facilities. With rapidly developing technology, it's important to keep hard assets and equipment up to date and in good repair. Downtime can be costly and in the long run cost more than regular upgrades. This doesn't mean everything has to be top of the line, just appropriate for the work to be done and for people to feel good about their work environment.

Beyond corporate facilities and equipment, each employee needs up to date hardware, software, systems and applications to do their jobs well. This is very important for morale, enhances productivity and profits, and makes a more positive impression on customers and prospects. Treat you employees the way you would like to be treated, for best results. And now, here's a closing note about facilities as a success factor.

You are judged by the company they see.

People, especially prospective customers, gain such a strong impression of your corporate personality (e.g., trustworthiness, professionalism) when they visit your space, it is very hard to undo any negative impressions. Now if your customer never visits your hole in the wall, no problem. But rather than "our work speaks for itself," unfortunately research has shown that your place of business speaks such volumes that your prospect may never get past that powerful perception of your space.

Generally lawyers, accountants and physicians who charge big bucks all know this. And if you want to come across as the low-cost provider, you don't need or want leather chairs or oriental rugs. But that doesn't mean your customer or prospect is going to enjoy sitting in your waiting room in a chair that feels and smells like a sweaty dog or sliding across your dirty brown linoleum floor to meet with you.

If you need new or improved space, I highly recommend hiring an experienced architect. The best ones are interested not only in designing your new building or expansion, but in helping you manage your facility throughout its lifecycle. If you are leasing office or retail space in a multi-tenant building, the right architect can make your interiors shine, attract customers, and help retain employees – an excellent return on investment.

Interrelationships with Other Success Factors

Finally, as a checklist for ensuring effective 21st-Century **financial management**, consider its interrelationships with the other Key Success Factors with questions like these:

- Do our finances reflect our overall **strategy** for the future, and are improvement initiatives adequately funded? Will planned changes increase our profits and financial strength? How?
- Do our finances reflect the needs and concerns of our **people**, and have we allowed for the recruitment and retention of talented people?
- Do our financial plans reflect the needs of our **markets**, as determined by objective research or surveys into the needs, perceptions and preferences of customers, prospects, and others outside of the organization?
- Have we considered the financial aspects of our **operations**, how we are going to pay for planned improvements, how operations can increase income and profits, and how operations can help ensure the continuing financial strength of the organization?

Key Success Factor No. 5: Finances – Chapter Summary

1. Plan for the capital and cash flow you will need to be successful.
2. Maintain competitive pricing to ensure customer value.
3. Use sophisticated financial controls to monitor cash flow and ensure profits.
4. Top management understands and tracks key financial data.
5. Use modular and flexible pricing so customers have choices.
6. Know the real costs of products/services so real profits are achieve
7. Each employee understands how his/her performance impacts profits.
8. Align financial rewards with results – not just longevity.
9. Retain sufficient earnings to balance out economic cycles.
10. Provide adequate facilities and equipment for the work to be done.

Putting It All Together In A Total Business Success System

The time has come to combine all 5 Key Success Factors into an integrated system to maximize your success, what we call a **Total Business Success System.** The Total Business Success System (TBSS) is best illustrated with this diagram, which we introduced earlier in this book:

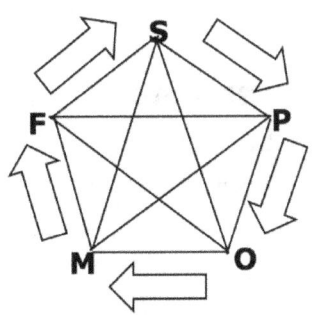

Here you see the **5 Key Success Factors** arranged in a star formation, with arrows indicating a predominant flow. The point is to demonstrate that all factors are interrelated, with connections to all the other factors at the same time. But actually it does not matter that much how we illustrate the 5 factors – which one is on top, which one comes next – since this is a simplification of complex reality, and all factors are interconnected in three dimensional space plus time. Here's how this understanding can help you:

1. Your organization functions as a total system.

This means it is a whole which is greater than the sum of its parts, whether you want it to or not. All the parts are connected and interdependent. If something happens to one, it affects the others, and so forth. You cannot work on one of these Success Factors effectively without acknowledging its linkages with the others. For example, Strategy should be developed with the input of your People and Markets, among other constituents.

2. For optimum success, it is essential to have all five success factors congruent.

Most importantly your <u>people</u> and <u>operations</u> need to be congruent with what <u>customers</u> want and need. *Congruent* means "having mutual agreement or conformity." A popular way to say this is "in sync." Operations should be designed to produce value for customers, and people should be focused on creating that value – and continuously improving it. Strategy is the overarching big plan, but unless it is aligned with your finances, you will have problems. If you reflect on this diagram and think about the relationships between each pair of Success Factors, you begin to see how this can be a guide to action. It's simple enough to remember, but complex enough to deal with a wide variety of situations and challenges.

3. Remember to have all the key factors covered.

In developing your strategic or long-range plans, this Total Success System diagram can serve as a planning guide. I once worked with a client group who had a lot of ideas which we began putting on the board. Then we sorted the ideas into the 5 Key Success Factors and found out that there was not one single point related to the organization's people! Some of them were participating in the meeting, but no one voiced how important it was to include people/staff development/training in the strategic plan. A corollary of this is, everything you manage or control can be put into one of these 5 Success Factor "buckets" if you understand them adequately.

4. Consider the value of cross-functional teams.

When you go to implement a plan of any kind, you run into the problem that certain issues or responsibilities affect everybody and cannot be neatly pigeonholed into an existing functional department like manufacturing, sales or service. In industry it is increasingly common to deal with these problems through organizing cross-functional teams representing different areas of the company.

One effective way to do this is to divide your people up into five teams, one for each Success Factor. If you have enough people, consider posting a sign-up sheet in the break room or on your intranet and let people sign up for what they are interested in. If you're a nonprofit, mix up board members, staff and volunteers on the five teams so they can work together on broad issues.

However you organize, make sure you have these 5 bases covered. The Strategy team can include the chairs of the other 4 groups plus the CEO, or it can be a group unto itself. Again this framework helps ensure that everything important gets covered and that there is a group already in place for every cross-functional or large problem which comes up.

As Albert Einstein said, "Everything should be as simple as possible, but no simpler." The Total Success System is just such a solution – about as simple as you can get, but (or should we say therefore) very powerful.

We hope you have enjoyed learning about the 5 Key Success Factors of Business Success and the underlying action principles. And we hope you use this information for your own greater success!

If you did enjoy this book, we would really appreciate your leaving a favorable review on amazon, as explained below. That will increase its visibility on the site and make it more likely others will enjoy the book as well.

You can also reach me, the author, at BuckLawrimore.com or LCIweb.com (Leadership Counseling Institute).

Here's to your great success in business and life!

Please Leave A Review

If you enjoyed reading this book, please leave a review on amazon.com:

1. Go to the product detail page for this book. If you've placed an order for the book, you can also go to <u>Your Orders</u>.
2. Click **Write a customer review** in the Customer Reviews section.
3. Select a Star Rating (we appreciate 5 stars).
   A green check mark shows for successfully submitted ratings.
4. (Optional) Add text, photos, or videos and click **Submit**.

Thanks in advance for your review!

Now, please enjoy our 3 Appendix sections which follow.

Appendix 1: The SimpleD Decision-Making Model

Decision-making is a primary component of wisdom and the very essence of being human. We all have to make thousands of decisions every day. Many decisions are automatic or happen so fast we aren't even aware of the decision-making process. In this appendix we are going to explain a little about decision-making and our "SimpleD" model for decision-making, developed and refined over a number of years to be highly useful and easy to remember.

Making good decisions can lead to greater success and a better life. Making bad decisions can lead to problems, pain, failure and even disasters.

We cannot always know the consequences of our decisions. For example, a visitor to our community was trying to find her destination and made a quick turn into a side street. She did not see the biker beside her, but in an instant she killed the biker, with enormous painful consequences for both families and others.

Our minds use an ancient, fast, decision-making process designed to protect us from danger like an approaching tiger and instantly decide friend or foe, fight or flight. This allowed our species and others to survive and thrive for millions of years. But it is not always helpful in today's complex, connected world. In fact it is often counter-productive

Decision Making First Principle: Think Before You Act

The first and most important principle in good decision-making is, **"Think before you act."** As noted above, our minds evolved to react to danger so we could survive. The first rule of animal survival is, "Don't get killed." In fact this react-to-survive response is hardwired into the brains of all animals with brains – or they would not be here in our world today.

This primitive part of the brain, called the reptilian or lizard brain, is a complex mass of tissue at the top of our spinal column. It evolved eons before the rest of the brain. But it still calls the shots much of the time, especially under pressure! Most of our decisions are made so fast we don't even stop and think. The general principle of "Think before you act" is easy to say but hard to do.

So you will be doing yourself a big favor, as well as those who are close to you, if, whenever possible you learn to check yourself before you jump to a conclusion or take an action. Now if a child runs out in front of your car, you need to slam on the brakes before you can consciously think about it. But if you need to decide what to have for dinner, it would be better to think about it first, including to ask your spouse, partner or others who might be eating that meal. And of course if you need to make a larger decision like how to save for retirement, far more thought and research is needed. More on this below.

Decision Making – From Boy To Terminator

Making better decisions is something that has interested me my entire life. As a boy, my stepfather sometimes criticized me by asking, "Why didn't you think?" I have always been prone, like a lot of people, to act quickly and often impulsively unless I knew I had lots of time to decide. Many of my mistakes in life were made by not thinking carefully before acting. Of course when you are young, you don't even know how to think systematically, and some people never learn how.

In college I majored in philosophy and psychology, partly to learn better ways of thinking and to understand how the mind works. Although my career veered into journalism, public relations and marketing, I have continued to read hundreds of books and thousands of articles on decision-making, wisdom and how the mind works. The best of this has been useful in my personal life and business consulting.

The main problem with most decision-making models is that they were designed for business, and in many cases for group decision-making. That is certainly important, and the entire fortunes of companies often rise or fall based on the decisions made. Many books about decision making are also long and involved – too much to remember and use for everyday life.

But the Simple D decision-making model was developed not only for business applications but also in hopes that it will make your life a little better. For that to happen, its core methodology has to be very simple, so simple you can memorize it, keep it in your head, and use it to think through any situation or challenge without pulling out paper or a smartphone to write on.

Albert Einstein once said, "Everything should be as simple as possible, but no simpler." When it comes to a useful decision-making model, we could not agree more. If the model is too complicated, you are much less likely to use it. But if it is too simple, you would soon find it is not very useful for making important decisions well.

The 80-20 rule says that 80 percent of the value comes from 20 percent of the content. So we tried to eliminate the less valuable 80 percent and find and refine the 20 percent that is truly valuable and useful for you whether in business or personal life.

If you saw the early *Terminator* movies starring Arnold Schwarzenegger, there were a number of scenes "inside the head" of the Terminator as it calculated the situation with little screens in the field of view before making a decision. This was the director's way of sharing what the Terminator was thinking without having him speak aloud about it. This has long been my visual inspiration for a better way to make quick decisions without jumping to conclusions – a little chart or table we can carry in our heads to help make better decisions. After years of working on this, I came up with the Simple D Decision- Making Model. Here's how it works.

The Simple Decision- Making (SimpleD) Model

First we will present the Simple Decision-Making (SimpleD) Model, then explain each of its components, to help you understand and use it. We have intentionally transformed other more obvious words into S-i-m-p-l-e-D (pronounced "Simple D") to provide an easy aid to memory. It isn't perfect or all encompassing, but it is easy to remember and recall in your mind without having to pull out a smartphone or sheet of paper.

Now let's look at each component separately.

- **Situation** – Decision Making Step 1

The situation is what you are facing as you try to make your decision. The time you spend analyzing your situation should be proportionate to the importance and urgency of the situation. You probably can handle a decision about what to have for dinner with a 30-second discussion with your partner, if any. But if you are trying to decide which house to buy, you should obviously do much more fact-finding.

An easy way to remember what to consider is the 5W2H question list from journalism and news reporting:

- **Who** – is involved?
- **What** – is going on?
- **When** – is this happening – time frame?
- **Where** – is this happening – location?
- **Why** – is this happening – apparent causes?
- **How** – is this happening – process?
- **How much** – is involved in terms of money and time?

If you are in a big hurry (really) just answer the question: "I need to make a decision about …" and put it into a few words for yourself.

- **Intentions** – Decision Making Step 2

This is what you want to accomplish in this situation. For example, if you were an offensive football coach, you would need to decide about what play to run next. Your intentions would be to make a first down, score, and ultimately win the game.

If you need to decide about what to eat for dinner, your intentions might be to have a satisfying meal, to prepare and consume it in a short amount of time, and not to spend much money. Or in another situation your intentions might be to go to a fine restaurant, impress your date, and strengthen your relationship. It all depends on your situation.

Getting clarity on your intentions is very important. It will have great impact on your decision-making and the value of it.

If you are in a hurry, just ask yourself, "What am I trying to accomplish?" If you have a little more time, there are four main types of intentions:

- **Purposes** – Rarely do we have just one purpose when trying to make a decision. If you take a few minutes, you can ask yourself why, why, why – up to 5 times – to clarify your purposes. And then you might want to take the fourth or fifth "why" and make it your No. 1 purpose. For example, let's say you are planning dinner with your significant other. Your obvious purpose might be, "So we can have something to eat." Why? "So we can nourish our bodies and fill our stomachs." Why? "So we can take care of our health." Why? "So we can live longer and better." Or maybe your train of thought goes to "So we can have a romantic evening" and then "So we can strengthen our relationship" etc.

- **Visions** – Sometimes when we are trying to make a decision, we have a picture or vision in our heads of the desired outcome. Again maybe it is a picture of a romantic evening or of being healthy and strong. Making your intention visual is very helpful, as long as you keep in mind that this is a "rough draft" subject to further decision-making steps.

- **Values** – What is most important to you? What personal values are relevant here? Maybe health values, financial values, emotional values, spiritual values, moral values, ethical values? We recommend that you take a few minutes right now to write down your most important values so they are in recent memory when you need to think about your decision-making intentions.

- **Inclusion** – If there is one thing that leads to bad consequences in decision-making, it is failing to include others in the process. Again if you have only 60 seconds to decide, the other person(s) might not be there with you for a quick conversation. Of course you can pick up your smartphone and probably get an answer to "Honey, what do you think about this?" in a heartbeat, but this needs to be a learned habit for many people, including me. If you have time, just ask yourself, Who will likely be impacted by this decision? Then see if there is any way you can get their input before you decide, before it's too late, before a long string of painful consequences starts to unwind just because you were in a big hurry. When in doubt, ask before you jump.

- **Multiple Options** – Decision Making Step 3

If you are in a hurry to make a good decision, your options are going to be limited. Your options for what to have for dinner could be to eat from the freezer or order take-out. (Or theoretically your dining options could include driving to another city or hiring a caterer, but those are going to take more time and probably more money than you want to invest.) If you are considering buying a new house and living in a medium-size or larger city, you might have dozens of housing options, depending on your income and local housing costs. You might not like or want them all, but there will be plenty of them out there. So again the number of options you create needs to be relevant and appropriate for the situation you are in.

If you're doing this in your head or chatting with a partner, you might limit your options to three. If you have a little more time, you might need to jot them down on a sheet of paper or a smartphone app. If you have even more time, you might want to do an online search to see what options are out there.

Here's a short personal story about how options can evolve as you explore. Not long ago one of our Siamese cats started licking herself in a few spots so intensely, she licked off all the hair and even part of her skin. The underlying tissue looked like raw hamburger, and we were quite concerned. We had to research optional cures online and calling our vet because this was something we had never encountered before.

Unfortunately none of these initial "solutions" worked, but a friend suggested we try CBD oil. We bought some in liquid form – very expensive – but were not sure how much to give the cat, since this was a human "drug." So we called the manufacturer, who offered very kindly to send us some samples of CBD ointment for free, something we had never heard of. The ointment worked like magic, rapidly healing all her wounds and breaking the habit entirely! This is a good example of how you don't always know your options at first, and others will evolve if you keep looking and trying.

If you have time, let your brain generate some new options overnight before you decide. You'd be amazed how creative your brain can be if you just give it a question in the evening and let it process it overnight or later in the day. Sometimes the best options come to us while taking a shower, driving a car or other activity that does not put too much demand on our higher mental powers.

So now you have your list of options – short, long or evolving, depending on the situation. How do you weigh each option so you can move your decision-making forward?

- **Pros-Cons** – Decision Making Step 4

One of the best ways to evaluate each option was first popularized by Benjamin Franklin in the 1700s and is still very useful today. Create two columns on a sheet of paper, spreadsheet or other app. Across the top (header row) put the name of the option in a few words, and in one column list the "pros" or positives, and in the next column list the "cons" or negatives. If you have multiple options now, this might be hard to do in your head. It would be difficult to keep all the points in active memory. But this is why good intentions often lead to bad decisions – not taking time to think through the options.

Actually this is how our brains work automatically as we make a decision. Millions of neurons rapidly process the known options and the one with the most "votes" gets selected. A quarterback has only a few seconds running the Run-Pass Option (RPO) to decide what to do with the football. He rapidly scans the field and moving bodies and makes an instant decision. This rapid option-weighing no doubt developed over millions of years as our brains considered the fight-or-flight option upon spotting a large animal moving toward our ancestors in the brush.

But we can get better results today by taking appropriate time to think about multiple pros and cons for each option. This can take up more than one sheet of paper, but paper is cheap and spreadsheet space is free. In the process of identifying a "pro" you might then be able to come up with a "con" that is the opposite. For example "fast service" might be contrasted with "higher cost." Don't just look at the pros-cons list once but think about each item and try to come up with more possibilities now or overnight.

- **Long View** – Decision Making Step 5

When we take the long view, we think about possible consequences. Jeff Bezos, Amazon founder and one of the world's richest men, has said that he likes to think about what the consequences of a decision might be 20 years from now. This is another huge pitfall that causes a lot of "good now" decisions to go "bad later." Your Pros-Cons list can help you get started on this, but often that is in the present, and the future cannot be clearly predicted. One of billionaire Warren Buffet's favorite sayings is, "It is better to be roughly correct than precisely wrong." You are going to have to do some guesswork to take the long view and ultimately some risk. Practically all decisions involve some risk, and one characteristic of wise people is the capacity to take the long view and the risk.

Just take a few minutes to imagine each of your main options as a movie, and run the movie forward into the future. It's surprisingly easy to do and can even be fun. Some things like fine wine get better with time, and some things like fresh fruit rot (unless they are turned into wine of course). Some things that are affordable now can get more and more costly each year – housing and taxes are good examples.

Once I had a summer romance with a college girl two years younger than me. She lived in Mississippi and I, a recent college graduate, lived in North Carolina. We met at a mountain retreat center when I was working as a news reporter. We were quickly attracted to each other, and I came back at the end of the summer to drive her back home to Mississippi. That was definitely a "heart over head" decision. On the long way home in an old car without air conditioning, I took the long view and realized this relationship could not be sustained for the two more years she needed to complete college. The long view is always a wise choice before making an important decision.

- **Evaluation** – Decision Making Step 6

You've weighed your options and now is the time to look them over and evaluate which one is best. If you've done this on paper or a spreadsheet, it should be fairly obvious. By now you probably have a gut feeling or intuition about the best route to take. Even if you've done this in your head riding down the road or sitting in a chair or going for a walk, evaluation is so much easier when we've thought through our intentions, multiple options, pros and cons, and the long view.

One way to simplify the evaluation step is to distribute 100 percentage points, representing your time, money or energy, over the options. For example if you had four options and one was preferred, you might score them 75, 15, 10, 10. This is totally subjective for each situation and process.

- **Decision** – Decision Making Step 7

The word "decision" comes from Latin roots meaning "to cut off." Make the decision, cut off other options, and move on. After all your careful preparation and analysis, this becomes more a matter of will, of not second-guessing yourself, than any complicated process. You can clarify this by defining next steps which you will take following your decision. This might include actions you'll take, observations or measurements to make, and allowance for corrections or feedback to give you satisfaction and useful results.

We hope you find that it works for you, in business and life.

Appendix 2 - Starting Your Own Business

Starting a business from scratch involves a lot of time and information, more than we have room for in this book, which as we have said, is focused on the 5 Key Success Factors and related action principles. We have touched on several business start-up concepts earlier, and we also provide a substantial amount of information about running a successful business throughout this book. In this Appendix, we'll hit the high spots of what starting a new business entails.

Do what the market needs, not just what you like

All too many small businesses begin with a favorite interest or hobby of the owner, and this is one reason so many fail. Approximately 20 percent of new businesses fail during their first two years, 45 percent during the first five years, and 65 percent during the first 10 years. Only 25 percent of new businesses make it to 15 years or more. Don't start a business failure. Find out what the market needs first.

You can do this through online research to identify businesses if any already operating in your target market area. Are they satisfying the market demand for their products or services, or is there a need for what you want to offer?

Ask your friends and acquaintances, especially ones that will tell you the truth, what they think of your business idea.

If you can't afford to hire a market research firm to test your new business idea, check with your local college or university to see if they have marketing or research classes that might want to do a survey for you at no cost.

If you are brave enough, contact a few companies that are in the business you want to enter, play the bright-eyed novice, and ask them how they got started and what advice they would offer.

I remember when my marketing agency was young, I got a call from a would-be entrepreneur who wanted to start his own ad agency, wondering if I would meet with him and share some of my insights. Since we were not really an ad agency, I agreed, as did other agency owners, and he became quite successful. (I would never do that today because the business is so much more competitive, but you never know what response you'll get till you ask).

Remember: Do what the market needs, not just what you like, and be willing to abandon or drastically modify your idea if the facts warrant it.

Follow SBA business plan guidelines

The website SBA.gov, operated by the Small Business Administration, is chock full of ideas and guidelines about how to start your own business. As these words are written, their home page has a main feature entitled "Start your business in 10 steps" with a red button labeled SEE THE GUIDE. Go there and get it and read it.

The SBA is a big advocate of creating a business plan before you start your business, and provides valuable information how to create one. It directs you to think through all the costs involved in starting and running your business, and when the cash flow might come in. You can do this using an Excel spreadsheet, imagining month by month how your business will first need to spend money before it makes money, and so how much start-up capital you would likely need. Then double that estimate, because all newbies tend to be overly optimistic and naive about what business costs will be.

After you create your business plan, contact your local community college or Chamber of Commerce to see if someone who is more experienced will look at it with you and give you feedback to make it more realistic. This service is often provided free of charge and is very valuable.

Use market segmentation and product differentiation

Years ago I learned that the four most important words in business success, especially marketing, are *market segmentation* and *product differentiation*. This is such great advice that unfortunately many start-ups do not know and so do not follow, often leading to serious problems.

Market segmentation means selecting your target market in terms of demographics such as age, income level, location, or in the case of selling to businesses, consider number of employees, annual sales and other metrics. One of life's great truths regarding business is this: You can't be all things to all people. The more you focus on a segment or part of the marketplace where you might have a competitive advantage, the more likely you will succeed.

Product differentiation means your product is not a copycat but is different in a way that will matter to customers – *the difference that makes the difference*. If your local bakeries are all selling American-style cakes, maybe you want to offer Asian-style pastries. If other local lawn services offer mow-and-blow, maybe you offer a high-tech service with a website that allows customer to select special services such as fertilizing, reseeding, or mulching. Focus on product differentiation that is a natural fit for your personality and strengths, something you already know how to do or could quickly learn to give you a competitive advantage.

Treat all employees and customers with caring and respect

Tim Sanders once wrote a highly-rated book called *Love Is the Killer App: How to Win Business and Influence Friends*[4]. And boy, was he right! Genuinely caring for your employees and customers pays strong dividends. Employees are more likely to perform better and stay with you. Customers are more likely to be loyal, keep buying from you, and over the years pay you a huge amount of money.

This is a success secret many people don't appreciate. Some people think you must be tough in business and protect your rights. Well, that is important, but it needs to always be balanced with the caring aspect, which should be dominant in your decisions to enjoy the benefits mentioned above.

Appendix 3: Christian Business Success - Guiding Principles

Christian business success involves juggling a complex set of challenges that at times conflict with each other. But if you follow the principles and guidelines outlined below, you too can achieve Christian business success.

Let's begin by getting clear what "Christian business success" means. Taken literally, it means:

- Christian – a follower of Christ and his teachings
- Business – an organization which generates income by creating value for customers and selling products or services
- Success – achieving an objective; often used to include wealth, fame, and influence

An online search reveals that a number of famous business leaders, including some multimillionaires, were openly Christian and tried to follow Christian principles and practices in their business. According to research by GiantsForGod.com, these highly successful leaders and their companies include:

- John D Rockefeller Sr - Standard Oil
- David Green - Hobby Lobby
- Tom Monaghan - Domino's Pizza
- S Truett Cathy - Chick-Fil-A
- Sir John Templeton - Mutual Fund Pioneer
- Norm Miller - Interstate Batteries
- Anthony Rossi - Tropicana
- Asa Candler - Coca Cola
- Henry Parsons Crowell - Quaker Oats
- Marion Wade - Service Master
- Bo Pilgrim - Pilgrim's Pride
- Bud Paxson - Home Shopping Network
- Stanley Tam - US Plastic

But it might be a mistake to set your hopes on achieving this kind of fame and fortune if you want Christian business success. Each person benefited from being at the right place at the right time and working very hard to achieve business success. Did being a Christian make them more successful? Did God help them succeed? We do not know. The point is, there is no guarantee that being a Christian and even doing everything you can to love and obey God will make you a success in business. This gets to the crux of the matter.

"Christian business success" is not an outright contradiction or oxymoron, but it includes a tension which must be realized if you want to be a success both in business and as a Christian.

The Old Testament taught that obeying God would lead to prosperity, and it was believed that prosperous people were favored by God. Here for example are a few relevant *Old Testament* quotes:

- Psalm 25:13 – "His soul will abide in prosperity, And his descendants will inherit the land."
- Proverbs 28:25 – "An arrogant man stirs up strife, But he who trusts in the LORD will prosper."
- Proverbs 13:21 – "Adversity pursues sinners, But the righteous will be rewarded with prosperity."
- Psalm 37:11 – "But the humble will inherit the land And will delight themselves in abundant prosperity."
- Joshua 1:8 – "This book of the law shall not depart from your mouth, but you shall meditate on it day and night, so that you may be careful to do according to all that is written in it; for then you will make your way prosperous, and then you will have success."

But in the New Testament we read that Jesus said:

- Matthew 19:24 – "And again I say unto you, It is easier for a camel to go through the eye of a needle, than for a rich man to enter into the kingdom of God."
- Mark 10:21 – Speaking to the "rich young ruler," "And Jesus, looking upon him, loved him, and He said to him, You lack one thing; go and sell all you have and give [the money] to the poor, and you will

have treasure in heaven; and come [and] accompany Me [walking the same road that I walk]."

- Matthew 6:24 – "No one can serve two masters. Either you will hate the one and love the other, or you will be devoted to the one and despise the other. You cannot serve both God and money."

Yet ever since the Garden of Eden, we humans have had to toil to survive. This is no less true today in our era of computers and automation than it was 5,000 years ago. The Bible refers to Jesus' vocation in only one verse – Mark 6:3 – "Is not this the carpenter, the son of Mary and brother of James and Joses, and Juda and Simon?" But scholars have since determined that the Greek word previously translated as "carpenter" is more accurately translated as "stone mason" or simply "builder." And indeed many passages in the New Testament refer to buildings and stone masonry. Most buildings in ancient Galilee were built of stone, not stick-built with wood as many are today in the U.S. Either way, the implication is that Jesus worked for a living before he became an itinerant evangelist.

The same is true for the 12 Apostles, many of whom were fishermen.

In Acts 18:3 we learn that the Apostle "Paul went to visit them, and he stayed and worked with them because they were tentmakers by trade, just as he was." We do not know if this was a major source of income for him, because elsewhere in his letters he talks about how members of various churches provided him and his partners with financial support. But again we can say, at some point in his life, Paul also worked for a living.

Life is not the Garden of Eden, and money does not grow on trees. Unless you win the lottery, or inherit a lot of money from a relative, or you marry someone who makes a lot of money and you don't have to, then you are going to have to work to make a living. Given that fact, there is no way we can say that business success is contrary to Christian faith. This leads to several important considerations about Christian business success:

- **Christian business success is neither good nor bad –** *how you achieve it is the key*. You can have a thriving business selling addictive drugs, or importing clothing made with slave labor, or treating your employees harshly. But such behavior is contrary to Christian principles. You can make or sell almost any product or service in a legitimate manner, paying fair prices for supplies or materials, and treating your employees with respect and Christian love.

- **The Bible is not a substitute for learning about and using smart business practices.** The Bible is about our relationship to God and our fellow human beings, about right living and strong principles. It is not the source of all knowledge. It will not tell you how to operate a computer or a car, how to create a website or a brochure, how to win a football game, how to cook spaghetti, or many of the thousands of skills and knowledge sets we must master to be successful in life and business.

- **The business world is a competitive arena, a jungle, where only the fittest survive and thrive.** You cannot achieve business success just by opening your doors and hoping customers come in and buy. As the saying goes, "Hope is not a strategy." You can ask God to guide you and help you, but He is not going to zap all relevant business knowledge into your brain with a lightning bolt from heaven. You have to learn before you earn. And fundamentally you have to provide the right product at the right price in the right place with superior service – better than your competitors do. It's tough running a successful business, and most of them fail in the first few years as a result. The Bible says to love your enemies, but that does not mean when a potential customer contacts you that you have to send them to your competitors instead. Being a good Christian in business does not mean being stupid or self-defeating.

- **Christian love is a phenomenal practice to enhance business success.** Every human being wants to be loved, respected, and treated fairly. You can treat your customers with Christian love by taking time to understand their needs, modifying your products and services to meet those needs, and communicating with them honestly that you are now offering exactly what they want. This is actually the essence of what is called *the marketing orientation* – putting customers first. There is tremendous power in building and refining your business to provide exactly what customers want – and to constantly adapt to changing needs and market conditions.

In the same manner, Christian love is a wonderful way to relate to and care for your employees or team members. Try to understand their needs and unique abilities. Help them develop their talents to become more productive and successful. Make them your full partners in taking care of customers. Establish a strong set of values, vision and mission statements, goals and strategies built on Christian principles and the enthusiastic participation of everyone in your organization, business, or team. Monitor their performance and give them loving but honest feedback to help them continuously improve, just as the organization strives to continuously improve.

In these ways Christian faith and love actually become competitive advantages, combining with business acumen to develop an ever-stronger organization with happy customers and happy employees, meeting real needs and earning market dominance as a result.

To learn more about Christian faith and practice in business, we recommend that you read the Bible and any number of good books and Christian commentaries. One book we recommend is *Success God's Way* by Charles Stanley. We also write about Christian faith at our website, Faitheos.com.

About the Author

E. W. "Buck" Lawrimore is a life-long writer, editor, publisher, and success consultant. He began writing for daily newspapers in high school, served as a correspondent for The Charlotte Observer while attending Davidson College, and graduated with a degree in psychology and minor in philosophy. He then went to work for The Charlotte Observer full-time as a reporter and editor.

Subsequently he returned to Davidson to serve as Director of the News Bureau, a position he held with various titles until 1979. He helped the college achieve increased national recognition, won a national award for his public relations work, and founded WDAV, a leading classical music radio station.

He then launched Lawrimore Communications Inc., a strategic marketing, communications and business consulting firm. Over 40 years, the firm served hundreds of business, government, and nonprofit clients, helping them achieve millions of dollars in additional sales and income, improved brand awareness, and many other success goals. The agency's brand slogan was "Creative Strategies for Your Success" and the firm developed many creative strategies to help clients be more successful. Mr. Lawrimore also studied and consulted on *key success factors* for many organizations and individuals during that time. He currently serves as president of the Leadership Counseling Institute (LCIweb.com).

He is the author of 10 other books, mainly on success in business and life, strategic planning, and philosophy, all available on amazon.com. Or visit https://amazon.com/author/bucklawrimore . He can be reached through his various websites, including LCIweb.com and BuckLawrimore.com. At this writing, LCIweb.com is a noted resource on "the five key success factors of business" based on high search engine rankings.

Bibliography

Following are some of the many books whose concepts were incorporated into the *5 Key Success Factors of Business* system:

Ackoff, Russell L. (1999). *Ackoff's Best: His Classic Writings on Management.* Wiley.

Ackoff, Russell L. (1999). *Re-Creating the Corporation: A Design of Organizations for the 21st Century.* Oxford University Press.

Ariely, Dan. (2008). *Predictably Irrational: The Hidden Forces That Shape Our Decisions.* HarperCollins.

Baer, Jay. (2013). *Youtility: Why Smart Marketing Is about Help Not Hype.* Portfolio.

Barker, Eric. (2017). *Barking Up the Wrong Tree: The Surprising Science Behind Why Everything You Know About Success Is (Mostly) Wrong.* Harper One.

Barrett, Lisa Feldman. (2018). *How Emotions Are Made: The Secret Life of the Brain.* Mariner Books.

Barrett, Newt. (2008). *Get Content. Get Customers. How to use content marketing to deliver relevant, valuable, and compelling information that turns prospects into buyers.* Voyager Media.

Battram, Arthur. (2002). *Navigating Complexity: The Essential Guide to Complexity theory in Business and Management.* Spiro Press.

Bechtell, Michele L. (1995). *The Management Compass: Steering the Corporation Using Hoshin Planning.* American Management Association.

Bradford Ph.D., David, Robin Ph.D., Carole. (2021). *Connect: Building Exceptional Relationships with Family, Friends, and Colleagues.* Currency.

Bradford, Robert W. (2000). *Simplified Strategic Planning: The No-Nonsense Guide for Busy People Who Want Results Fast.* Chandler House Press.

Brown, Mark Graham. (1996). *Keeping Score: Using the Right Metrics to Drive World-Class Performance.* Quality Resources & AMACOM.

Buckingham, Marcus, & Coffman, Curt. (1999). *First, Break All The Rules: What the World's Greatest Managers Do Differently.* Simon & Schuster.

Buckingham, Marcus, and Clifton, Donald O. Ph. D. (2001). *Now, Discover Your Strengths.* Free Press.

Burchard, Brandon. (2017). *High Performance Habits: How Extraordinary People Become That Way.* Hay House.

Buzzell, Robert D., and Gale, Bradley T. (1987). *The PIMS Principles (Profit Impact of Market Strategy): Linking Strategy to Performance.* Free Press.

Christensen, Clayton M. (2003). *The Innovator's Solution: Creating and Sustaining Successful Growth.* Harvard Business School Press.

Cialdini, Robert B. (1984). *Influence: The Psychology of Persuasion.* Quill.

Collins, James C., and Porras, Jerry L. (1994). *Built to Last: Successful Habits of Visionary Companies.* HarperBusiness.

Cross, Dick. (2012). *Just Run It! Running an Exceptional Business Is Easier Than You Think.* Bibliomotion.

Dalio, Ray. (2019). *Principles: Life And Work.* Simon & Schuster.

Damani, Ravi; Damani, Chetan; Farbo, Dana, and Linton, Jane. (2005). *Online Marketing.* Imano.

Davison, Ron. (2011). *The Fourth Economy: Inventing Western Civilization.* Ron Davison.

Dawson, Ross. (2005) *Developing Knowledge-Based Client Relationships: The Future of Professional Services.* Routledge.

Day, George S. (1990). *Market Driven Strategy: Processes for Creating Value.* Free Press.

De Geus, Arie. (2002). *The Living Company.* Harvard Business Review Press.

Drucker, Peter F. (1964). *Managing for Results.* Harper & Row.

Drucker, Peter F. (1973). *Management: Tasks, Responsibilities, Practices.* Harper & Row.

Eisenberg, Bryan. (2006). *Waiting for Your Cat to Bark?: Persuading Customers When They Ignore Marketing.* Thomas Nelson.

Franz, Peter, and Kirchmer, Mathias. (2012). *Value-Driven Business Process Management: The Value-Switch for Lasting Competitive Advantage.* McGraw-Hill.

Fulmer, William E. (2000). *Shaping the Adaptive Organization: Landscapes, Learning, and Leadership in Volatile Times.* AMACOM.

Gale, Bradley T. (1994). *Managing Customer Value: Creating Quality and Service that Customers Can See.* Free Press.

Gerber, Michael E. (1995). *The E-Myth Revisited: Why Most Small Businesses Don't Work and What to Do About It.* HarperCollins.

Gerber, Michael E. (1998). *The E-Myth Manager: Why Management Doesn't Work – And What to do About It.* HarperBusiness.

Gerber, Michael E. (2007) *E-Myth Mastery: The Seven Essential Disciplines for Building a World Class Company.* HarperBusiness.

Gharajedaghi, Jamshid. (1999). *Systems Thinking: Managing Chaos and Complexity: A Platform for Designing Business Architecture.* Butterworth Heinemann.

Hall, Kindra. (2019). *Stories that Stick: How Storytelling Can Captivate Customers, Influence Audiences, and Transform Your Business.* HarperCollins.

Hammond, John S. (2002). *Smart Choices: A Practical Guide to Making Better Decisions.* Crown Business.

Haroun, Chris. (2015). *101 Crucial Lessons They Don't Teach You in Business School.* Haroun Ventures.

Harper, Stephen C. (1991). *The McGraw-Hill Guide to Starting Your Own Business: A Step-by-Step Blueprint for the First Time Entrepreneur.* McGraw-Hill.

Harpst, Gary. (2008). *Six Disciplines® Execution Revolution: Solving the One Business Problem That Makes Solving All Other Problems Easier.* Six Disciplines Publishing.

Heath, Chip, and Heath, Dan. (2013) *Decisive: How to Make Better Choices in Life and Work.* Currency.

Hiebeler, Robert. (1998). *Best Practices: Building Your Business with Customer Focused Solutions.* Simon & Schuster.

Hughes, Mark. (2005). *Buzzmarketing: Get People to Talk About Your Stuff.* Portfolio Hardcover.

Kaplan, Robert S., and Norton, David P. (1996). *The Balanced Scorecard: Translating Strategy Into Action.* Harvard Business Review Press.

Kawasaki, Guy, and Fitzpatrick, Peg. (2014). *The Art of Social Media: Power Tips for Power Users.* Portfolio.

Keirsey, David, and Bates, Marilyn. (1984). *Please Understand Me.* Gnosology Books.

Kotter, John P. (2012). *Leading Change.* Harvard Business Review Press.

Labovitz, George, and Rosansky, Victor. (1997). *The Power of Alignment: How Great Companies Stay Centered and Accomplish Extraordinary Things.* Wiley.

LeBlanc, Mark. (2003). *Growing Your Business!* Expert Publishing, Inc.

LeBoeuf, Michael, Ph.D. (1985). *The Greatest Management Principle In The World.* Putnam.

Liker, Jeffrey. (2004). *The Toyota Way: 14 Management Principles from the World's Greatest Manufacturer.* McGraw-Hill.

Lissack, Michael. (1999). *The Next Common Sense: Mastering Corporate Complexity Through Coherence.* Unknown.

Massey, Morris. (1979). *The People Puzzle: Understanding Yourself & Others.* Reston Publishing.

McCandless, Keith, and Lipmanowicz, Henri. (2014). *The Surprising Power of Liberating Structures: Simple Rules to Unleash A Culture of Innovation.* Self-published.

McMaster, Michael. (1994). *Precision: A New Approach to Communication: How to Get the Information You Need to Get Results.* Grinder, DeLozier & Associates.

Meadows, Donella H., and Wright Diana. (2008). *Thinking in Systems: A Primer.* Chelsea Green Publishing.

Mihaescu, Constantin. (2014). *Small Business Process Management Guidelines: New Systemic Vision Using The Universal Model of Organization.* Kindle.

Miller, James Grier. (1965). *Living Systems, 1st Edition.* Delta Education.

Mintzberg, Henry. (1994). *The Rise and Fall of Strategic Planning.* Free Press.

Moody, Paul. (1983). *Decision Making: Proven Methods for Better Decisions.* McGraw-Hill.

Moore, Geoffrey A. (2014). *Crossing the Chasm, 3rd Edition: Marketing and Selling Disruptive Products to Mainstream Customers.* Collins Business Essentials.

Myers, Gail E., and Myers, Michelle T. (1985). *The Dynamics of Human Communication.* McGraw-Hill.

Nadler, Gerald, Ph.D., and Hibino, Shozo, Ph. D. (1998). *Breakthrough Thinking: The Seven Principles of Creative Problem Solving.* Prima Publishing.

Newman, David. (2013) *Do It! Marketing: 77 Instant-Action Ideas to Boost Sales, Maximize Profits, and Crush Your Competition.* AMACOM.

Norman, Jan. (1999). *What No One Ever Tells You About Starting Your Own Business: Real Life Start-Up Advice from 101 Successful Entrepreneurs.* Dearborn Trade.

Odden, Lee. (2012). *Optimize: How to Attract and Engage More Customers by Integrating SEO, Social Media, and Content Marketing.* Wiley.

Olson, Edwin E., and Eoyang, Glenda H. (2001). *Facilitating Organization Change: Lessons from Complexity Science.* Wiley.

Open University, The. (2016). *Systems thinking and practices.* The Open University.

Oshry, Barry. (2007) *Seeing Systems: Unlocking the Mysteries of Organizational Life.* Penguin Random House.

Oshry, Barry. (1999). *Leading Systems: Lessons from the Power Lab.* Berrett-Koehler Publishers.

Panagacos, Theodore. (2012). *The Ultimate Guide to Business Process Management: Everything you need to know and how to apply it to your organization.* Self-published.

Pearman, Roger R. (1998). *Hard Wired Leadership: Unleashing the Power of Personality to Become a New Millennium Leader.* Davies-Black.

Peppers, Don, and Rogers, Martha, Ph.D. (1993). *The One To One Future: Building Relationships One Customer at a Time.* Crown Business.

Peters, Thomas J., and Waterman, Robert H. Jr. (1982). *In Search of Excellence: Lessons from America's Best-Run Companies.* Harper & Row.

Pfeffer, Jeffrey, and Sutton, Robert. (2000). *The Knowing-Doing Gap: How Smart Companies Turn Knowledge Into Action.* Harvard Business School Press.

Pink, Daniel H. (2012). *To Sell Is Human: The Surprising Truth About Moving Others.* Riverhead Books.

Pofeldt, Elaine. (2018). *The Million-Dollar, One-Person Business: Make Great Money. Work the Way You Like. Have the Life You Want.* Lorena Jones Books.

Porter, Michael E. (1980). *Competitive Strategy: Techniques for Analyzing Industries and Competitors.* Free Press.

Porter, Michael E. (1985). *Competitive Advantage: Creating and Sustaining Superior Performance.* Free Press.

Rackham, Neil. (1988). *SPIN Selling.* McGraw-Hill.

Ries, Al, and Trout, Jack. (1981). *Positioning: The Battle for Your Mind.* Warner Books.

Rifkin, Jeremy. (2014). *The Zero Marginal Cost Society: The Internet of Things, the Collaborative Commons, and the Eclipse of Capitalism.* St. Martin's Press.

Robert, Michel. (1995). *Product Innovation Strategy, Pure and Simple: How Winning Companies Outpace Their Competitors.* McGraw-Hill.

Ross, Aaron, and Tyler, Marylou. (2011). *Predictable Revenue: Turn Your Business Into a Sales Machine with the $100 Million Best Practices of Salesforce.com.* PebbleStorm.

Senge, Peter. (2006). *The Fifth Discipline: The Art and Practice of the Learning Organization, Second Edition.* Image Books.

Shaw, Patricia. (2002). *Changing Conversations in Organizations: A Complexity Approach to Change (Complexity and Emergence In Organizations Series).* Routledge.

Spence, John. (2009). *Awesomely Simple: Essential Business Strategies for Turning Ideas Into Action.* Jossey-Bass.

Stacey, Ralph. (1996). *Complexity and Creativity in Organizations.* Berrett-Koehler Publishers.

Stacey, Ralph. (2001). *Complex Responsive Processes in Organizations: Learning and Knowledge Creation (Complexity and Emergence in Organizations Series).* Routledge.

Stephenson, James. (2003). *Entrepreneur Magazine's Ultimate Small Business Marketing Guide: Over 1500 Great Marketing Tricks That Will Drive Your Business Through the Roof.* Entrepreneur Press.

Thomas, Kenneth W. (2000). *Intrinsic Motivation at Work: Building Energy and Commitment.* Berrett-Koehler Publishers.

Treacy, Michael, and Wiersema, Fred. (1995). *The Discipline of Market Leaders: Choose Your Customers, Narrow Your Focus, Dominate Your Market.* Addison-Wesley.

Tzu, Sun. (1983). James Clavell, Ed. *The Art of War.* Delacorte Press.

Vaynerchuk, Gary. (2021). *Twelve and a Half: Leveraging the Emotional Ingredients Necessary for Business Success Leveraging the Emotional Ingredients Necessary for Business Success.* HarperBusiness.

Watzlawick, Paul; Beavin, Janet Holmin; and Jackson, Don D. (1967). *Pragmatics of Human Communication: Interactional Patterns, Pathologies and Paradoxes.* Norton.

White, Sarah-Jane. (2011). *49 Quick Ways to Market Your Business for Free: An Instant Guide to Marketing Success.* Harriman House.

Whiteley, Richard, and Hessan, Diane. (1997). *Customer-Centered Growth: Five Proven Strategies for Building Competitive Advantage.* Perseus Books.

Yohn, Denise Lee. (2014). *What Great Brands Do: The Seven Brand-Building Principles that Separate the Best from the Rest.* Jossey-Bass.

Zaltman, Gerald. (2003). *How Customers Think: Essential Insights into the Mind of the Market.* Harvard Business School Press.

Zeithaml, Valerie A., Parasuraman, A., and Berry, Leonard L. (1990). *Delivering Quality Service: Balancing Customer Perceptions and Expectations.* Free Press.

End Notes

---

[1] https://www.truity.com/?a=53464 – this is an affiliate link but has no connection to my recommending Truity. Their basic test is free.

[2] Available at LCIweb.com.

[3] https://www.truity.com/?a=53464 – this is an affiliate link but has no connection to my recommending Truity. Their basic test is free.

[4] Available on amazon.com at https://amzn.to/3y3RRkk